Training for Speed, Agility, and Quickness

Second Edition

Lee E. Brown

Vance A. Ferrigno

Editors

Human Kinetics

Library of Congress Cataloging-in-Publication Data

Training for speed, agility, and quickness / Lee E. Brown Vance A. Ferrigno editors.-- 2nd ed.
  p. cm.
  Includes bibliographical references.
  ISBN 0-7360-5873-7 (soft cover)
  1. Physical education and training. 2. Speed. 3. Motor ability. 4. Coaching (Athletics) I. Brown, Lee E. II. Ferrigno, Vance, 1961-
  GV711.5.T72 2005
  613.7'11--dc22

                    2005008059

ISBN-10: 0-7360-5873-7
ISBN-13: 978-0-7360-5873-5

Developmental Editor: Leigh Keylock
Assistant Editor: Carla Zych
Copyeditor: Andrew Smith
Proofreader: Sarah Wiseman
Permission Manager: Carly Breeding
Graphic Designer: Andrew Tietz
Graphic Artist: Francine Hamerski
Photo Manager: Dan Wendt
Cover Designer: Keith Blomberg
Photographer (cover): Chris Edwards
Photographer (interior): Chris Edwards, unless otherwise noted
Art Manager and Illustrator: Kareema McLendon
Printer: United Graphics

Human Kinetics books are available at special discounts for bulk purchase. Special editions or book excerpts can also be created to specification. For details, contact the Special Sales Manager at Human Kinetics.

Printed in the United States of America   10

The paper in this book is certified under a sustainable forestry program.

Human Kinetics
Web site: www.HumanKinetics.com

United States: Human Kinetics
P.O. Box 5076
Champaign, IL 61825-5076
800-747-4457
e-mail: humank@hkusa.com

Canada: Human Kinetics
475 Devonshire Road, Unit 100
Windsor, ON N8Y 2L5
800-465-7301 (in Canada only)
e-mail: info@hkcanada.com

Europe: Human Kinetics
107 Bradford Road
Stanningley
Leeds LS28 6AT, United Kingdom
+44 (0)113 255 5665
e-mail: hk@hkeurope.com

Australia: Human Kinetics
57A Price Avenue
Lower Mitcham, South Australia 5062
08 8372 0999
e-mail: info@hkaustralia.com

New Zealand: Human Kinetics
Division of Sports Distributors NZ Ltd.
P.O. Box 300 226 Albany
North Shore City, Auckland
0064 9 448 1207
e-mail: info@humankinetics.co.nz

Contents

iii

Preface

Welcome to the second edition of *Training for Speed, Agility, and Quickness!*

As editors, it is our goal to create the ultimate resource for athletes and coaches looking to finesse their technique and proficiency in these critical areas.

In this edition, you'll find that we take extra steps to ensure the information presented is the latest, most complete information available. Our first step is to build on our success in the key areas of speed, agility, and quickness by adding sections on balance and reaction time. These areas are critical to athletic performance in all sports and empower athletes by giving them the required skills to excel physically. We think these additions help to round out the total athlete.

In addition to the added content, we've also created a supplemental DVD that takes the book's instructions even further by illustrating several of the more complex drills with video and sound. This enables you to watch for directions and cues. Specifically, the DVD enhances the strong drill instruction contained in the book by highlighting difficult aspects of drill performance and technique. The visual layout of the book displays drills in an easy-to-use format, and you can readily see when a drill includes DVD footage by the icon placed above the drill title. Since the drills are organized by category, you can also skip around the DVD at your leisure to look at the drills with which you need assistance.

Here are highlights of each chapter, including important DVD links.

• Chapter 1: This chapter discusses the important link between speed, agility, and quickness training and sport-specific training. It gives a primer on muscle physiology and the science behind the exercise strategies in the rest of the book.

• Chapter 2: It is here that we lay out the foundation of training. Testing of the athlete must take place before a detailed training program can be implemented. The coach must know where the athlete currently stands in his or her athletic achievement before prescribing drills to fix specific problems. Many of the assessments in this chapter are also illustrated on the DVD.

• Chapter 3: In this chapter, the science behind speed is explained along with the fundamentals of program design. Different aspects of speed are explored and a detailed list of drills and illustrations depict how to exercise for maximum performance. DVD highlights include coverage of complex drills and step-by-step instructions.

• Chapter 4: Agility and balance are covered here to display to the athlete the sorts of drills that improve one's ability to rapidly change directions while keeping the body in proper alignment. This is essential for the execution of cut-and-turn maneuvers, which are fundamental to a wide array of sports. DVD highlights include multiple-angle views of these drills so you can see from all sides the footwork that is so integral to agility and balance.

• Chapter 5: Finally, quickness and reaction time are discussed as they relate to the previous chapters. Often the difference between success and failure on the sporting field is directly related to an athlete's ability to anticipate another player's movements and therefore beat the other player to a particular spot. DVD highlights include both upper- and lower-body drills designed to enhance explosive speed either while moving or from a stationary position.

• Chapter 6: This chapter ties the whole book together by delivering a guideline to program design. The instructions will show you how to choose drills specifically for each sport and athlete. They include tables of preselected drills that the coach can freely modify to suit the needs of the athlete.

It's our hope that athletes and coaches incorporate the approach to speed, agility, and quickness recommended here into their training and reach new heights of athletic achievement in their individual sports.

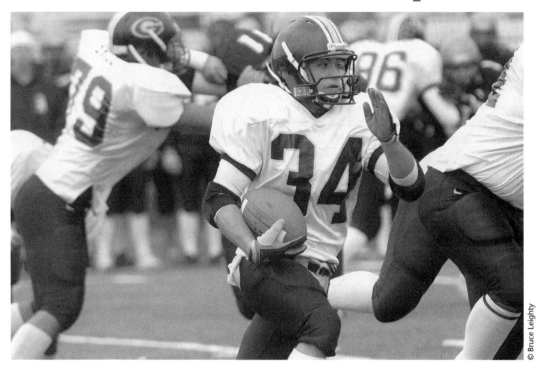

Chapter 1

© Bruce Leighty

How the Training Works

Lee E. Brown and Joshua Miller

Speed, agility, and quickness training has become a popular way to train athletes. With the continually increasing need to promote athletic ability, this type of training has proven to enhance the practical field abilities of participants in a wide variety of sports. It is practiced in addition to conventional resistance training in the gym and serves to assist in the transfer of the strength gained there to performance in the arena of play. Nearly every sport requires fast movements of either the arms or legs, and speed, agility, and quickness training can improve skill in precisely these areas. Hence, all athletes can benefit when speed, agility, and quickness training is integrated into their training program.

Although this type of training has been around for a number of years, many athletes have not practiced it. This is due primarily to a lack of education regarding both its specific benefits and how to integrate it into a complete training program.

In particular, speed, agility, and quickness training is intended to increase the ability to exert maximal force during high-speed movements. It manipulates and capitalizes on the stretch-shortening cycle (SSC) while bridging the gap between traditional resistance training and functional-specific movements. Some benefits of speed, agility, and quickness training include increased muscular power in all multiplanar movements, brain-signal efficiency, kinesthetic spatial awareness, motor skills, and reaction time. The acquisition of greater balance and reaction time will serve to allow the athlete to maintain proper body position during skill execution and react more proficiently to any change in the playing environment. Quick movements are useless if the athlete trips over his or her own feet.

Many athletes and coaches also do not realize that speed, agility, and quickness training can cover the complete spectrum of training intensity—from low to high. Each athlete will come into a training program at a different level, so the level of intensity must coincide with the athlete's abilities. For example, at the lower-intensity end of the spectrum, the assorted biomotor skills illustrated throughout this book can be used to teach movement, warm-up, or the basics of conditioning. No significant preparation is needed to participate at this level of speed, agility, and quickness training. Higher-intensity drills require a significant level of preparation. A simple approach to safe participation and increased effectiveness is to start a concurrent strength-training program when beginning speed, agility, and quickness training.

Let's review how speed, agility, and quickness training works and how it can be implemented within workouts for complete conditioning.

Understanding the Muscles at Work

Understanding the basic physiology of muscular function is invaluable to understanding why this particular type of training is so effective.

Within the body, each skeletal muscle is made up of connective tissue, muscle tissue, nerves, and blood vessels and is controlled by signals sent from the brain. These components work together in a coordinated fashion to cause bones and therefore limbs to move in desired patterns. Muscle tissue is connected to a tendon, which is a noncontractile length of tissue that connects the muscle to a bone. Thus, tension developed within the muscle transfers to an adjoining tendon and then to a bone.

On an even more intimate level, within each muscle fiber there are hundreds or even thousands of thin longitudinal fibers. These fibers contain two opposing contractile and fingerlike proteins called actin and myosin that form attachments called cross-bridges and pull against one another to cause motion. Through a series of chemical reactions controlled via brain signals, these proteins work to repeatedly pull and release. This causes muscular work, or a contraction, to occur.

The SSC is at the heart of speed, agility, and quickness training. It works like a rubber band that is stretched and then snaps back together and involves a combination of eccentric (muscle-lengthening) and concentric (muscle-shortening) actions. An eccentric muscle action is performed when an athlete lowers a weight, such as during the downward movement in a biceps curl or a squat exercise. A concentric muscle action occurs during the upward, or opposite, movement in the above exercises. When an eccentric action precedes a concentric action, the resulting force output of the concentric action is increased. This is the essence both of the

SSC and speed, agility, and quickness training. Examples of SSC in sports occur with the swing of a baseball bat or a golf club, during which an individual precedes the intended motion with a wind-up or prestretch. Without this eccentric action, or if there is a pause between this action and the follow-through, the increased force output that is supposed to occur during the concentric phase of the exercise will not occur. The SSC also takes place during everyday activities, such as walking and running, yet is greatly intensified during speed, agility, and quickness training.

Advantages derived from the SSC can be seen in both large and small ways at all levels of sporting competition. One example is with the vertical jump. When the jumper precedes his or her jump by bending at the knees and hips and then explodes upward, the resultant jump height will be greater than performing the same movement by stopping at the bottom of the knee bend for a few seconds before the explosion portion of the jump. Another example can be seen in the baseball pitch. If the pitcher does not complete a wind-up, he or she is unable to generate as much force as would be possible by performing a prestretch motion.

SSC activities can be done for the upper body as well as for the lower body and can be implemented with external devices, such as free weights, rubber tubing, and medicine balls. Devices such as these assist the athlete in performing both the concentric and eccentric portions of the exercise insofar as they need either to be accelerated or decelerated. However, speed, agility, and quickness training may be performed without assistive devices by simply using one's own body mass as the weight or resistance.

Integrating Speed, Agility, and Quickness Training

It is very important to remember that speed, agility, and quickness training is designed to supplement traditional resistance training. In other words, it should be conducted in addition to and not instead of lifting weights. Speed, agility, and quickness training at higher intensities should begin after a solid foundation of general conditioning has been established. This could mean six months to a year of foundational training for a beginner. The main point is to have enough of a strength base to adequately complete each speed, agility, and quickness exercise without undue strain. In addition, high-intensity speed, agility, and quickness training should normally be undertaken during the month or two just prior to the season and should include no more than 2 days per week and 30 to 45 minutes per session of total activity.

When writing an exercise program for any athlete, you need to take many parameters into consideration. First, consider years of training, level of fitness, and how often the athlete will be performing speed, agility, and quickness training. In addition to these considerations, three important training variables need to be discussed. They are frequency, intensity, and volume.

Frequency, Intensity, and Volume

Training frequency refers to the number of training sessions completed in a given amount of time, usually per week. Intensity applies to the quality of work performed during muscular activity and is measured in terms of power output (that is, work performed per unit of time). Training intensity may also be defined as how easy or difficult a particular activity is. Finally, volume describes the quantity or the total number of sets and repetitions completed in a training session. These three factors, combined with the number of years an athlete has trained and his or her fitness level, all go into making up the training plan for the athlete.

We can divide athletes into three major categories: novice, experienced, and advanced. The novice athlete is just beginning to exercise for sport. He or she might be an adolescent athlete or even an adult who chooses to take up sport later in life. The novice athlete's potential for improvement is great. The experienced athlete has been training for one to five years and is involved in a regular program of exercise and sport. Although competing at a higher level, he or she still has great opportunity for improvement. The advanced athlete competes at the national or international level at which events are decided by inches or hundredths of a second. These athletes are near their genetic limits; therefore their potential for improvement is small and the details of their program must be precise. Training age (number of years training for a sport) is more meaningful than chronological age in categorizing the athlete.

For the novice athlete planning an integrated program, begin by adding one to two basic speed, agility, and quickness training exercises into the current training schedule. In particular, it is important that athletes begin with the basic techniques of each exercise before advancing to their more technical aspects. Furthermore, learning the proper mechanics of more basic exercises will allow the athlete to progress to advanced exercises in a timelier manner. As the novice athlete becomes more advanced, his or her frequency of training also will increase: from two to three times per week. Remember that as the athlete progresses, there still must be rest days to allow for the muscles to recover. Coaches may employ different programs that allow for 2 or 3 days off per week. As the athlete gets closer to competition, however, that number is likely to decrease.

The athlete should always begin each exercise at a low to moderate intensity and progress slowly while learning new movements, decreasing the total number of repetitions as intensity level is increased. Progression from low to super-high intensity may depend on which part of the training year the athlete is in. The intensity level is generally lower at some times during the year to make sure that the athlete is able to perform the prescribed exercise correctly while also avoiding injury. Low intensity may consist of performing the exercises at 40 to 50 percent of maximal exertion. Moderate intensity would constitute an increase to between 50 and 80 percent, and high intensity to between 80 and 100 percent, of maximal exertion.

Intensity and volume directly influence one another in that as intensity increases volume must decrease. Early in the program volume is high while intensity is low. As the athlete nears competition, volume is decreased as intensity increases. Measuring training volume (number of sets × number of repetitions) is vital for assessing training progression. How great a volume of training is performed within a given training session is based on the athlete's level of fitness. The proper interaction of the number of sets and repetitions with variation in training intensity may also help augment training adaptations. These adaptations become evident through repeated training sessions. Upon progressing to a desired fitness level, always allow the athlete to adequately recover.

Periodization

One way to design a program that maximizes the components of frequency, intensity, and volume is through periodization. Periodization involves the gradual cyclical alteration of frequency, intensity, and volume of training throughout the year to achieve peak levels of fitness for the most important competitions. It organizes the annual training program into specific phases during which the athlete trains in varying ways to meet objectives particular to each phase. Thus, all the phases of a periodized program together constitute a macrocycle. On its own, in turn, each phase constitutes a mesocycle, which may stretch over several weeks or months, depending on the goals set by the athlete and coach. The mesocycle may be further separated into even smaller sections called microcycles, which are generally periods of training that last around one week, depending on the type of event for which the athlete is preparing.

Safety Considerations and Injury Prevention

An appropriate warm-up session should precede every exercise session. Warm-up routines should begin with a low-intensity whole-body activity, such as jogging. This will increase heart rate and blood flow to the muscles and tendons, thereby preparing the athlete for the higher-intensity workout to come. This general warm-up should be followed by a specific warm-up that consists of performing some of the session's exercises at a low intensity.

Injury prevention is a major part of any training program. It is imperative that every athlete advance in a progressive and systematic manner when embarking on such a program, including speed, agility, and quickness training. A properly conducted strength-training program that emphasizes knee, hip, back, and ankle strength will reduce the possibility of injury when speed, agility, and quickness training is first introduced. Training should progress from simple to complex movements, from low to high intensity, and from general to sport-specific motor patterns. Moreover, factors such as frequency, intensity, volume, body structure, sport specificity, training age, and phase of periodization should always be considered when designing speed, agility, and quickness training.

Here are a few more recommendations for injury prevention: Follow the proper progression of exercises, and wear proper clothing and shoes.

Remember, proper safety procedures must be observed while learning and mastering the speed, agility, and quickness activities included in this book. Make certain all equipment is in correct working order before use. If exercising outdoors, make sure the area is free of any hazardous objects, such as rocks or trees. Be sure to understand each new exercise completely prior to attempting it for the first time.

It is also important to make mention of a common occurrence experienced by athletes. When one first attempts a new exercise, there is likely to be muscle soreness. This soreness, called *delayed onset muscle soreness* (DOMS), usually peaks between 24 and 72 hours after the exercise bout. The eccentric portion of the exercise (described earlier) is the primary cause of DOMS, and the prevailing explanation for DOMS is micromuscle tears. This has been observed in studies utilizing an electron microscope to reveal tissue damage in the fibers. The only way to reduce the development of DOMS is to adapt to the exercise stress. This requires repeating exercise bouts over several weeks with sufficient rest between sessions. Since all speed, agility, and quickness training involves eccentric exercise utilizing the SSC, it is recommended that novice athletes perform no more than two exercise sessions per week separated by 2 or 3 days. Experienced and advanced athletes may perform up to 3 days per week.

In summary, speed, agility, and quickness training is high-intensity work that requires a foundation of strength before implementation. It may result in mild muscle soreness until the athlete adapts to prescribed exercises. Therefore, these exercises should be introduced slowly before progressing to higher intensity and greater complexity. In the coming chapters, we will describe the drills that make up speed, agility, and quickness training and show how to integrate them into a complete training plan. But first we will discuss methods for assessing athletes' fitness levels and skills.

Chapter 2

© Empics

Athlete Assessment

Steve Plisk

The first step in designing a training program is to conduct an evaluation of the athlete and his or her competitive activity. In training circles, this evaluation is called a needs analysis, and its purpose is to obtain the initial information required to set training program variables, such as frequency, intensity, volume, and rest. In order to develop a program specifically tailored to an athlete's needs, a needs analysis for speed, agility, and quickness training should assess a number of factors. The principle factors to assess are the athlete's level of functional strength, his or her competency with movement mechanics, and the metabolic demands of the activity he or she will be performing.

Assessing Functional Strength, Movement, and Metabolic Demands

An athlete needs a basic level of functional strength in order to progress into speed, agility, and quickness training. Functional strength is used to produce force and power during athletic activities. Competency with movement mechanics, or the proper coordination of the body and its muscle groups, is required to skillfully execute techniques integral to these activities. An evaluation of the metabolic demands of the sport in which the athlete will participate is important to appropriately structure his or her speed, agility, and quickness training. Does the activity require short 10-second bursts of energy or several minutes of sustained motion? Once these factors are considered, exercises and drills can be chosen and training sessions developed to assure that the athlete is in peak form at the right time. The tests recommended in this chapter are summarized on page 16. A disk icon appears next to descriptions of tests that are demonstrated on the DVD.

Functional Strength

What follows are four distinctive approaches to evaluating an athlete's functional strength. Which speed, agility, and quickness exercises the athlete should perform relates not only to his or her abilities but, more importantly, to his or her level of experience. With this in mind, the first two methods of evaluation, identifying basic strength and reactive resources, are appropriate for novice and intermediate-level athletes. The latter two methods, assessing strength deficit and speed-strength, can be used with advanced athletes.

Basic Strength   It is commonly proposed that athletes should be able to squat one and a half to two times their body weight before performing advanced shock-type plyometric movements, such as depth or drop jumps (Zatsiorsky 1995). Due to the basic mechanical similarities between plyometric and agility exercises, this guideline is a useful starting point but not a requirement. The ability to perform a single-leg squat (as well as to lunge forward, laterally, or backward) is also a useful and practical prerequisite. Hence, evaluating how well such exercises are performed proves invaluable when assessing unilateral strength and basic movement competency.

Reactive Resources   The concept of reactive resources should not be confused with that of reaction time, which will be discussed in chapter 5. Measurement of reactive strength resources (Schmidtbleicher 1985a, 1985b, and 1992) involves comparing squat jump performance with drop jumps from heights of 16, 24, 32, 40, 48, and possibly 56 centimeters, depending on the athlete's competency (Schmidtbleicher, personal communication). A novice athlete's best drop jump performance may be 20 to 25 percent below his or her squat jump. This indicates large reactive resources, which means the athlete has a functional deficit in his or her short-response stretch-shortening-cycle abilities. In this case, speed, agility, and quickness training should focus on exercises that can improve reactive movements, such as drop jumps, vertical jumps, and countermovement jumps. In contrast, an advanced athlete's drop jump result may be up to 20 to 25 percent greater than his or her squat jump, indicating small reactive resources. With this situation, basic strength should be emphasized through hypertrophic (increasing the size of a muscle) and/or neural adaptations in order to create new reactive resources.

Strength Deficit An eccentric–concentric strength deficit is the difference between absolute (eccentric) strength and maximum (concentric) strength (Zatsiorsky 1995). This gives a sense of an athlete's ability to use his or her strength potential in a given motor task. A large deficit (for example, up to 45 percent) reveals that explosive exercises should be emphasized in order to improve neuromuscular activation. A small deficit (such as 5 percent) indicates that hypertrophic methods should be emphasized, followed by maximal heavy efforts.

Eccentric strength measurement can be problematic when a force plate, as is found in biomechanics laboratories, is not used. However, eccentric strength can still be approximated outside the lab by measuring the maximum load that can be lowered under control for 3 to 5 seconds during, for example, a squat (Siff 2003). It is advisable to evaluate each leg independently.

Speed-Strength Examples of control test norms for different sports and qualification levels are listed in tables 2.1 through 2.4. Discretion must be used when attempting to generalize performance expectations from one sport to another. Using football as an example, it may be tempting to infer that an interior lineman's abilities should match those of a weightlifter or that a perimeter player's skills should match those of a sprinter. These types of assumptions, however, can lead to misdirected training.

Table 2.1 Explosive Power Test Scores Among College Athletes

Test	MALES			FEMALES		
	Average	**Good**	**Elite**	**Average**	**Good**	**Elite**
30-m dash	3.9-4.1	3.6-3.9	3.3-3.6	4.5-5.0	4.2-4.5	3.8-4.2
30-m dash (flying start)	3.5-3.7	3.2-3.5	2.8-3.2	4.0-4.4	3.7-4.0	3.4-3.7
5 double-leg bounds	13.1-13.7	13.7-14.9	14.9-16.7	9.2-11.0	11.0-12.8	12.8-15.2
5 single-leg bounds	11.3-12.5	12.5-13.7	13.7-15.3	10.1-11.3	11.3-12.5	12.5-13.7
Backward overhead weight throw	11.6-12.8	12.8-16.4	16.4-19.8	6.7-9.1	9.2-12.2	12.2-15.2

Adapted, by permission, from R.W. Field, 1991, "Explosive power test scores among male and female college athletes," *National Strength & Conditioning Association Journal* 13(3): 50.

Running times are indicated in seconds and bounding/throwing distances in meters. Data are based on a small sample of NCAA Division I and II athletes (numbering 42) but provide some basis upon which to evaluate test performance.

Table 2.2 Controls for Sprinters

Test	100-M TIME					
	12.8-13.2	**12.3-12.7**	**11.8-12.2**	**11.2-11.7**	**10.7-11.1**	**10.2-10.6**
60-m dash	7.95-8.15	7.65-7.95	7.35-7.65	6.95-7.35	6.55-6.85	6.25-6.65
30-m dash	5.0-5.1	4.6-5.0	4.45-4.65	4.1-4.4	3.85-4.15	3.65-3.85
30-m (flying start)	3.9-4.0	3.6-3.8	3.4-3.5	3.05-3.35	2.8-3.0	2.55-2.75
Long jump	2.3-2.6	2.4-2.7	2.5-2.8	2.6-2.9	2.7-3.0	2.9-3.2
Vertical jump	0.39-0.47	0.46-0.54	0.53-0.61	0.60-0.69	0.68-0.77	0.76-0.85
3 bounds	6.8-7.4	7.2-7.8	7.5-8.1	7.9-8.5	8.5-9.1	9.2-10.0
5 bounds	12.2-13.2	12.8-13.8	13.4-14.4	14.0-15.0	14.6-15.6	15.9-17.1
10 bounds	19-29	21-31	23-33	25-35	27-37	29.5-39.5

Adapted, by permission, from F.W. Dick, 1987, *Sprints and Relays* (Birmingham: UK Athletics).

Running times are indicated in seconds and jumping/bounding distances in meters. Data represent a loose guide and given performances may be achieved without meeting all criteria.

Table 2.3 Control Tests and Norms for Elite Weightlifters

Test	BODY WEIGHT									
	52	**56**	**60**	**67.5**	**75**	**82.5**	**90**	**100**	**110**	**Over 110**
60-m dash	7.9	7.8	7.7	7.6	7.6	7.7	7.8	7.9	7.9	8.0
5 long jumps	12	13	13.5	14	14	13.5	13.5	13.5	13.5	13
Backward overhead weight throw (7.5 kg; juniors 5.0 kg)	11	12	13	14.5	14.5	14.5	14.5	15	15	14.5
Power snatch	85-100	95-115	110-125	120-135	125-140	135-150	145-160	155-170	160-180	170-190
Power clean	110-125	120-135	130-155	155-170	160-180	170-190	180-200	190-210	200-220	205-230
Back squat	170-190	180-200	200-220	210-230	220-240	230-250	240-260	260-280	270-290	275-300
Front squat	150-165	155-170	170-190	180-200	200-230	210-240	220-260	240-260	245-265	252.5-262.5

Adapted, by permission, from Professor Tamas Aján and Professor Lazar Baroga, 1988, *Weightlifting—Fitness for All Sports* (Budapest: International Weightlifting Federation).

Running times are indicated in seconds, jumping/throwing distances in meters, and weights in kilograms.

Table 2.4 Fitness Characteristics for NCAA Division I and II Football Players

Test	POSITION							
	QB	**RB/FB**	**TE**	**WR**	**OL**	**DL**	**LB**	**DB**
36.6-m (40-yd) dash								
Division I	4.70	4.55	4.80	4.49	5.17	4.89	4.67	4.53
Division I	4.70	4.53	4.78	4.48	5.12	4.85	4.64	4.52
Division II	4.81	4.69	4.84	4.59	5.25	5.03	4.76	4.61
Vertical jump								
Division I	79.6	86.1	78.9	88.7	68.6	77.1	83.2	88.1
Division I	80.7	85.9	79.6	87.4	68.8	77.9	83.2	87.8
Division II	70.3	74.2	70.1	77.8	60.4	66.9	72.4	78.0
Power clean								
Division I	124.6	138.3	140.9	127.5	143.4	146.8	144.3	127.1
Division II	120.0	127.3	122.6	123.5	132.0	132.7	131.6	116.1
Squat								
Division I	188.5	226.5	228.4	194.5	246.0	243.8	230.9	202.3
Division I	200.2	233.3	232.4	205.6	251.3	246.5	240.5	207.8
Division II	179.0	214.8	202.5	173.8	221.6	219.3	209.0	176.6
Bench press								
Division I	155.9	169.5	167.7	146.6	176.2	179.8	161.0	142.5
Division I	162.9	174.9	172.4	151.2	174.0	180.1	159.5	142.4
Division II	128.9	146.9	144.3	122.6	160.0	161.7	146.2	126.0

Adapted, by permission, from M.A. Garstecki, R.W. Latin, and M.M. Cuppett, 2004, "Comparison of selected physical fitness and performance variables between NCAA division I and II football players," *Journal of Strength & Conditioning Research* 18(2); adapted, by permission, from C.A. Secora, R.W. Latin, K.E. Berg, and J.M. Noble, 2004, "Comparison of physical performance characteristics of NCAA division I football players: 1987 and 2000," *Journal of Strength & Conditioning Research* 18(2).

Running times are indicated in seconds, jumping heights in centimeters, and weights in kilograms.

There is more information available on speed-strength and acceleration than on parameters for deceleration and agility. Once again, however, an important principle can be adapted from plyometric training (Zatsiorsky 1995). An athlete must be able to effectively decelerate from a given velocity in order to change direction, just as he or she must land safely and efficiently from a given drop height before attempting to do depth or rebound jumps from that height. Here is an example of how to progressively evaluate the ability to decelerate (Plisk 2000b):

1. The athlete achieves "second gear" (half speed) and then decelerates and stops within three to four steps.

2. Once the athlete can satisfactorily execute the first drill, a five- to six-step braking action from "third gear" (three-quarter speed) can be introduced.

3. Finally, a seven- to eight-step braking action from "fourth gear" (full speed) can be employed, if appropriate.

A similar approach can be applied to backward and lateral movements. While the choice of velocities and braking distances is somewhat arbitrary, it is imperative to establish each athlete's ability to decelerate from different speeds before attempting to redirect. As is the case with any athletic skill, this sort of training must be improved progressively with careful attention to movement mechanics in order to avoid injury.

Movement Competencies and Techniques

Athletes should possess the skill to accurately and successfully control their body movements in any fast-moving sporting activity. This is, of course, best accomplished through training undertaken with proper instruction. The following information describes some of these movements.

Sprinting Techniques and Mechanics

In contrast to some sports skills, sprinting is a natural activity that most athletes have experience with (whether or not their form is correct). Focus can often be directed toward perfecting form and correcting faults—while concurrently evaluating and developing an athlete's physical abilities—more so than on teaching new techniques. (Common technique errors and corrections are discussed on page 13.) This can be quite challenging, however, since it often involves changing established movement habits. While sprinting technique is addressed in more detail in chapter 3, some basic considerations are briefly addressed here.

There are three respective sprinting technique variants: *acceleration*, *transition*, and *maximum velocity* (Seagrave, personal communication). When applying each variant, three aspects of running mechanics are typically addressed: body position, including visual focus (the athlete should look in the direction that he or she intends to go); arm action (the athlete should facilitate leg action with aggressive hand and knee hammering or punching motions); and leg action (the athlete should move the legs explosively and minimize ground support time).

Agility Techniques and Mechanics

The dynamic balance, coordination, and explosiveness involved in agility movements present a unique technical challenge. A more detailed discussion of this issue is presented in chapter 4. But basic evaluation guidelines can be established by understanding running mechanics and drawing on practical experience (Gambetta 1996, 1997, Plisk 2000a, b).

Directional changes (for example, cutting left or right) and transitions (such as a "turn-and-run" maneuver from a backpedal into a forward sprint in the same direction) should be initiated by turning the head and focusing on a new target. This can be combined with appropriate footwork techniques, in this case an open or crossover step. Time and efficiency may be lost when the athlete begins by turning the shoulders or hips before the eyes and head, since this may result in rounding off a turn or weaving outside of a desired movement path.

The role of arm action while sprinting, especially during initial acceleration, also has important implications for agility. The athlete must quickly accelerate into a new movement pattern and a new path when executing transitions and turns. As is the case at the start of a sprint, explosive arm action in combination with good footwork technique should be used to rapidly get back up to speed. Inadequate or improper arm action may result in a loss of speed or efficiency.

Running Technique Errors

This checklist of common errors, and accompanying causes and corrections, can be used to evaluate running technique.

Insufficient leg extension at push-off (i.e., the athlete "sits")

Cause: Inadequate power transmission; push-off is not powerful enough and too hasty

Correction: Ankle joint work in forward movement; running and hopping, running and jumping, bouncing, special strengthening

Feet turned excessively outward

Cause: Faulty running form

Correction: Running in lane, walking, jogging, and slow running with feet turned slightly inward

"Bouncing" with marked vertical swaying

Cause: Push-off force directed too vertically

Correction: Longer push-off, hitting chalk marks at regular intervals, starting exercises, increased stride rate

Forward swing of lead leg is too wide; flat foot plant

Cause: Trunk/thigh weakness; fatigue

Correction: Snatching thigh in diagonal support (with and without additional load); high-knee lift under difficult conditions (e.g., in deep snow or sand, uphill, or with weighted footwear); strengthening exercises

Ineffective arm movements (transverse movement, excessive backward swing, hunched shoulders)

Cause: Excessive shoulder movement; insufficient shoulder-joint flexibility

Correction: Practice proper movements during easy stride, side-straddle position, or jogging

Head and neck hyperextended or hyperflexed

Cause: Fatigue; misunderstanding of movement

Correction: Normal erect head carriage, eyes focused ahead

Adapted, by permission, from G. Schmolinsky, 1993, *Track and Field: The East German Textbook of Athletics* (Toronto: Sports Books Publisher), 144-145.

Metabolic Demands

The metabolic demands of a sporting activity must also be considered when testing an athlete and designing a training program. The specific conditioning needed to properly execute the techniques involved in the activity at a level of effort achieved during competition is referred to as *special endurance* (Steinhofer 1997). It is a variation on the speed-endurance concept that originated among runners: the ability to maintain running speed after 1 to 2 seconds at maximal velocity, or to achieve maximum acceleration or speed during repetitive sprints.

The underlying strategy is to develop the physical and technical abilities needed to achieve a predetermined level of effort, or a target pace, in competition. The training implications for sports other than race events are relatively straightforward but infrequently applied.

The following five-step competition modeling checklist can be used to identify exercise-recovery patterns for most sports. This, in turn, can help to establish criteria for special endurance drills and tests (Plisk 2000a; Plisk and Gambetta 1997):

1. Identify the desired competition model with respect to several factors: level of competition, scheme/style/system of play, time periods, and personnel considerations.

2. Identify the nature and scope of competitive events with respect to intensity levels, as well as outcomes, goals, and objectives.

3. Videotape specific competitions or segments that meet criteria 1 and 2.

4. Evaluate these events according to basic exercise-recovery patterns, as well as any subdivisions and set-groupings (examples are provided in the following paragraphs).

5. Select core fitness training and testing drills according to workload intensity and duration, as well as any position- or situation-specific assignments and techniques.

Once a competition model has been identified, some important decisions need to be made regarding how to simulate efforts in training comparable to those needed in competition. Consider the following example of the preparation that can be taken for an NCAA Division I Final Four men's lacrosse competition. Looking specifically at the most demanding position in lacrosse, midfielder (Plisk and Stenersen 1992; Plisk 1994), most teams have three or four midfield units each of which plays 9 to 14 shifts per game (or about three per quarter). The average duration of a shift is 3 to 4 minutes with 5 to 9 minutes of subsequent recovery. Due to patterns in the start and stoppage of play, shifts can be further subdivided into six to eight work bouts averaging 32 seconds each in duration. NCAA rules dictate that play must resume within 20 seconds after each whistle (except following a goal or a timeout) and within 5 seconds of being signaled ready for play after a change of possession. Thus, a conditioning drill or test fit to imitate one quarter of play might involve three sets of seven 150-yard (137-meter) shuttle runs between two lines 25 yards (23 meters) apart. Each run should be 30 seconds in length and followed by 20 seconds of recovery time, and there should be 7 minutes of recovery time between sets.

A second example comes from NCAA Division I men's basketball (Taylor 2003 and 2004). A guard, for instance, averages 34.5 minutes of total playing time per game. He takes part, on average, in eight series per half, each about 2.5 minutes long and consisting of 19 to 22 intermittent work bouts. The average duration of these bouts is 8 to 9 seconds, with virtually none exceeding 20 seconds. About 47 percent of bouts involve high-intensity effort, with the remainder performed at submaximal effort levels. During each series there is usually one short recovery interval (25 to 40 seconds long) every 11 bouts, as well as one longer (50-second to 2-minute) timeout every 19 bouts. So a specific conditioning drill or test might involve several series of 22 shuttle runs from baseline to baseline and back through half-court, each taking at most 9 seconds to complete. Between repetitions, players should be allowed 15 seconds to jog to the baseline to line up for the next repetition. Two extended recovery intervals can also be included, one of 25 to 40 seconds after the 11th shuttle run and the other of 50 seconds to 2 minutes after the 19th (Taylor, personal communication).

Core training and testing drills can then be selected. Interval-type drills that fit the observed pattern of exercise and recovery provide a good starting point. Simple modifications of traditional ladder or line drills can also be appropriate, as are position-specific plays and tactical assignments.

Basketball and lacrosse were chosen to illustrate how variations in playing rules and strategies affect exercise and recovery patterns and overall metabolic demands. For example, aside from the obvious differences in the number of players and the total area of the two arenas of play, basketball players cannot substitute on the fly—as is allowed in lacrosse. The special endurance component of a needs analysis should address specific criteria in order to ensure that training and testing programs correspond to the demands of competition.

As we've seen, a needs analysis is the first step in designing effective training programs. The starting point for speed, agility, and quickness training is a three-pronged evaluation of an athlete's level of function strength, his or her competency with movement mechanics, and the metabolic demands of the activity he or she performs. In this way, the athlete's needs can be assessed and then matched to the corresponding drills in the following chapters. The goals of any program should be based entirely on the needs of the athlete and the requirements of the specific sport.

Speed, Agility, and Quickness Testing Checklist

Norms, when applicable, are presented in tables 2.1 through 2.4. In order to evaluate the athlete's level of preparation—and the effectiveness of a training program—test batteries that give valid, reliable, and objective results (but that are also easy to administer and interpret) should be planned.

Functional Strength

Basic Strength

- Ability to squat 1 1/2 to 2 times body weight
- Ability to single-leg squat body weight and to lunge (forward, laterally, and backward)

Reactive Resources

- Comparison of squat jump performance with drop jumps from heights of 16, 24, 32, 40, 48, and possibly 56 cm (depending on qualification level)

Strength Deficit

- Comparison of absolute involuntary eccentric strength (i.e., maximum load that can be lowered under control for 3 to 5 seconds) and maximum voluntary concentric strength

Speed-Strength

- Backward overhead weight throw
- 3, 5, or 10 bounds (double or single leg)
- 1 or 5 long jumps
- Power clean
- Power snatch
- Vertical jump

Movement Competencies and Techniques

Acceleration

- 30-m dash
- 30-m dash (flying start)
- 36.6-m (40-yd) dash
- 60-m dash

Agility

- 18.3-m (20-yd) shuttle
- 3-cone drill

Deceleration

- 2nd gear → 3- to 4-step braking action
- 3rd gear → 5- to 6-step braking action
- 4th gear → 7- to 8-step braking action

Movement Competency Assessment

- Motor skills
- Movement patterns

Running Technique/Errors

- Variables (drive, stride, lift)
- Mechanics (posture, arm action, leg action)

Metabolic Demands

Special Endurance Training Based on Tactical Modeling

- Core training/testing drill(s) selected according to competitive workload patterns as well as position- and/or situation-specific assignment(s) and technique(s)

Chapter 3

© Nigel Farrow

Speed Training

Doug Lentz and Andrew Hardyk

Hours spent developing speed through training ironically turn into a payoff that lasts only for a few seconds, even for world-class athletes. While most sports other than track sprinting do not offer the platform to showcase maximum running speed, sprint training lies at the foundation of numerous athletic activities.

Just think of how many critical game situations in various sports are won or lost by the ability to shift, when needed, into a higher gear. The bottom line is that a successful speed-training regimen can play a major role in making athletes more successful in many sports. The ability, for example, to speed up in order to chase down a free ball in a basketball game may make the difference between winning and losing. Unfortunately, many people subscribe to the philosophy that speed is something one is born with, not something that can be improved through training. So they spend little time on speed training. However, both experience and research have shown that a good speed development program can be incorporated into almost any workout regimen and can produce noticeable increases in speed.

To get maximum results from speed training, there are numerous factors to consider above and beyond pure genetic potential. These include stride length, stride frequency, strength, power, functional flexibility, acceleration, and proper technique. This chapter includes guidelines for speed development, drills for maximum speed attainment, and other matters of significance that contribute to improving speed.

Acceleration

For most sports, acceleration—the rate of change in velocity—is the most important component of speed development. In other words, being able to accelerate quickly means that the athlete can go from a stationary or near-stationary state to his or her maximum speed in a very short time. All athletes accelerate by increasing both stride length and stride frequency.

One way to increase stride length and stride frequency is to increase overall functional strength throughout the entire body. Improved strength levels will allow athletes to produce greater amounts of force while at the same time decreasing the time spent in contact with the ground. Training the body to use the attained strength gains in a powerful fashion is the key to improving acceleration. In a nutshell, the most powerful athletes spend less time in contact with the ground, have longer strides, and can take strides more rapidly than their less powerful counterparts.

The highest rates of acceleration are achieved in the first 8 to 10 strides taken by an athlete. Close to 75 percent of maximum running velocity is established within the first 10 yards (9 meters). Maximum running speed is reached within 4 to 5 seconds for most athletes.

To ensure a proper transition to top speed, quick running steps should gradually increase in length until full stride length is achieved. Explosive starting actions require the application of forces through the hip, knee, and ankle joints; and the execution of quick running steps requires tremendous elastic strength in the hip and knee musculature. Good mobility in the hip joint will assist athletes with leg separation during the "knee-lift" phase. Elastic strength prevents the leg from collapsing in the knee and hip regions during impact with the ground and also reduces the time that the foot is in contact with the ground.

Stride Frequency and Stride Length

The two main factors in running speed, as you might have guessed by now, are stride length and stride frequency. Increasing one or both will result in increased speed. However, they are interrelated in such a way that increasing one often results in the reduction of the other. For example, in an effort to increase stride length, an athlete may reach too far forward with the lower leg, resulting in overstriding. This decreases stride frequency, which results in a lower running speed. Good coaching is important to ensure that changes in stride length and frequency actually result in positive gains.

Stride frequency is measured by the number of strides taken in a given amount of time or over a given distance. By using good sprinting technique, stride frequency can be increased without sacrificing stride length. Increasing stride frequency is important because the athlete can only produce locomotive energy when his or her feet are in contact with the ground. The more often the feet touch the ground, the faster the potential running speed. This idea must be balanced with the fact that large amounts of force and power are necessary during the limited ground contact time in each stride. Modern sprint technique effectively maximizes this combination.

Sprint-assisted training is one technique that can be used to improve stride frequency. Assisted sprinting will allow athletes to develop the feel of running at a faster velocity than they would be capable of running normally. This added dimension of supramaximal speed enables athletes to improve their running mechanics at a faster rate than would be possible unassisted. By not having to run all-out but still being able to achieve a speed that is at or slightly above their unassisted best, athletes can learn to relax more easily at high speed. Some of the traditional assisted methods of training include downhill running and towing (see drills). To avoid injury, athletes should be well versed in the mechanics of proper sprinting form and adequately warmed up before attempting this type of training.

While stride frequency is calculated in terms of the number of steps taken per minute, stride length is the distance covered—measured from the center of mass—in one stride during running. Research has shown that optimal stride length at maximum speed is normally 2.3 to 2.5 times the athlete's leg length. A common mistake made by many young athletes is to try to take strides that are too long in an effort to attain or maintain top speed. When this happens, they have a tendency to overstride and ultimately slow themselves down because of decreased efficiency in force production. Most athletes develop their optimal stride length as proper technique and strength/power improve.

Stride length can be enhanced by improving sprint mechanics (see the following section on proper technique) and the athlete's power, absolute strength, and elastic strength through numerous forms of training. These include strength training; the use of weighted pants, weighted vests, running chutes, and harnesses; and uphill running (see drills). Coaches must be careful not to get too carried away with these different "resisted methods" of training. Overuse of these methods can adversely affect running technique, thereby undermining the overall process of speed development. Many books are available that discuss weight training and plyometrics in greater detail.

Proper Technique

Sprint mechanics is another term for sprint form or sprint technique. Proper mechanics allow the athlete to maximize the forces that the muscles are generating. This greatly improves the chances that an athlete will achieve the highest speed expected of him or her, given his or her genetic potential and training. Good technique also increases neuromuscular efficiency. This, in turn, allows for smooth and coordinated movements that also contribute to faster running speeds.

There are three main elements to concentrate on with regard to proper sprinting mechanics: posture, arm action, and leg action. Posture refers to the alignment of the body. An athlete's posture changes depending on which phase of the sprinting action he or she is in at a particular time. During acceleration, there is more of a pronounced lean (around 45 degrees from the horizontal plane). This aids in overcoming inertia. As the athlete approaches his or her maximum running speed, posture should become more erect (around 80 degrees). Regardless of the phase of sprinting, one should be able to draw a straight line from the ankle of the supporting leg through the knee, hip, torso, and head when the athlete's leg is fully extended just before the foot loses contact with the ground.

Arm action refers to the range of motion and velocity of the athlete's arms. The movement of the arms counteracts the rotational forces generated by the legs. Because these leg forces are substantial, vigorous and coordinated arm movements are necessary to keep the body in proper alignment. This is important in all phases of sprinting, but it is crucial in the initial acceleration phase.

Leg action refers to the relationship of the hips and legs relative to the torso and the ground. Making explosive starts and achieving maximum speed require extending the hip, knee, and ankle in a coordinated fashion to produce the greatest force possible against the ground. Also, in order to keep the stride frequency high and the stride length optimal, proper recovery mechanics—that is, what the leg does while it is not on the ground—are important.

When coaching speed mechanics, keep these other important factors in mind:

1. Head position: The head should be in line with the torso and the torso in line with the legs (at full extension) at all times. Do not allow the head to sway or jerk in any direction. Try to maintain a relaxed neutral position with the jaw relaxed and loose.

2. Body lean: Running can be seen as a controlled fall. As already mentioned, one should be able to draw a straight line through the body at full leg extension during each stride. The body should have a pronounced forward lean during initial acceleration, while at maximum speed it should be erect and tall. Concentrate on complete extension of the hip and knee joints as the foot pushes the body forward.

3. Leg action: The foot should remain in a dorsiflexed (toes up) position throughout the running cycle, except when the foot strikes the ground. At this point, the weight should be on the ball of the foot (never on the heel), directly under the athlete. As the foot leaves the ground, it follows a path straight up toward the buttocks. Simultaneously, the knee rises up and the thigh is almost parallel to the ground. The foot then drops down below the knee. At this point, the knee is at an angle of approximately 90 degrees. The leg aggressively straightens down and underneath the body to the ground contact point. This process is repeated over and over with each leg. The greater the running speed, the higher the heel should kick up. Failure to achieve a high rear-heel kick will reduce stride frequency, and the athlete should avoid placing the foot in front of the body when making contact with the ground. He or she should practice running as lightly and quietly as possible with correct foot-to-ground contact.

4. Arm action: Aggressive arm action is a must. Each arm should move as a whole, with the elbow bent at about 90 degrees. The hands remain relaxed, coming up to about nose level in the front of the body and passing the buttocks in the back. Arm action must always be directly forward and backward, never side to side. Arm swing should originate from the shoulder and not involve excessive flexion and extension of the elbows. The hands may be kept open or slightly closed, but always relaxed. The athlete should keep the thumb side of the hand pointed forward and up at all times during the movement; do not allow the wrist to move.

As top speed is approached,

1. the head is held high,
2. the torso becomes more upright,
3. the shoulders and head are relaxed,
4. the driving leg is fully extended to the ground, and
5. the heel of the recovery foot comes close to the gluteus.

Practicing the drills listed at the end of this chapter will improve proper technique, thus increasing running speed.

Developing Your Speed Potential

While there is no magic formula for developing or increasing maximum running speed, there are some specific guidelines that anyone can follow when training for speed improvement. Simply put, running brief and intense sprints with plenty of rest between repetitions is critical. Sound programs emphasize technique, starts, acceleration, speed endurance, and relaxation. Use these guidelines:

1. All speed workouts must be performed when the body is fully recovered from previous workouts. A tired, sore, or overtrained athlete cannot improve his or her speed capabilities. Therefore, speed training is most effective at the beginning of a workout session.

2. Proper sprinting technique must be taught to and mastered by athletes through the execution of many perfect drill repetitions over a long period of time. Speed does not come after one week of drills. It is derived over many months of hard work and hundreds of drill executions.

3. All sets and repetitions within a speed workout must be accompanied by adequate rest. The athlete's heart rate and respiration should return to almost normal levels from the previous drill. Any sprint drill that lasts 6 to 8 seconds, at a maximum or near-maximum effort, will have implications on the short-term energy system (ATP-CP) and the central nevous system. A one to four work-to-rest ratio is recommended as a good estimate.

4. Speed workouts should vary between light, medium, and heavy days. For example, back-to-back hard days would not be beneficial to speed enhancement. This would inhibit adequate recovery.

5. Track the total distance run by the athlete during each maximum speed workout.

6. To fully achieve maximum speed, the athlete must learn to run in a relaxed manner while at the same time producing maximum effort. This is much easier said than done, of course, especially with junior and senior high school athletes. Overexertion will produce extraneous body movements, which will detract from the power required to go fast.

7. Speed endurance can be accomplished by running longer intervals—165 to 440 yards (151 to 402 meters)—or by decreasing the rest between short intervals to between 20 and 65 yards (18 and 49 meters). The latter is a good choice for many sport-specific applications.

8. All speed workouts should be preceded by a dynamic warm-up and flexibility routine, which will prepare the athlete for maximum efforts.

It's important to pay close attention to the last guideline. A proper warm-up for sprint or acceleration training will prepare the athlete for the maximum efforts necessary for speed development. The purpose of the warm-up is to increase specific muscle and core body temperature. Good examples of an active warm-up routine include jogging (forward and backward), lunge walking, calisthenics, skipping, or any other aerobic activity. The general warm-up should typically be 5 to 10 minutes long with the goal being for the athlete to break a sweat. Generally, the warm-up should begin with slow, simple movements and move toward quicker, more complex movements.

After mild perspiration has been achieved, dynamic flexibility movements should follow. Dynamic stretching increases range of motion in the major joints utilized in sprint training and helps to stimulate the nervous system. Examples of dynamic flexibility include but are not limited to arm circles, trunk twists, stepping knee hugs, high kicks, lunging walks with rotations, walking on tiptoes, walking on the heels, ankle rotations, and leg swings. Another benefit to dynamic flexibility exercises is the variety available to coaches and athletes. We suggest mixing up the order occasionally, but ensure that athletes have hit the shoulders, torso, hips, quads, hamstrings, calves, and ankles. Dynamic flexibility routines should be 10 to 15 minutes in duration.

Recent research suggests that traditional static stretching impairs maximal force production and may even contribute to muscle injuries in dynamic activities that directly follow the stretching. Therefore, it is advisable to avoid these types of stretches until after all speed/power movements are completed—that is, at the end of the workout session during the cool-down.

Although true maximum speed may seldom be achieved in most sports settings outside of track, the ingredients that help to improve the times of track sprinters will work just as effectively for athletes in almost every sport. Many coaches and athletes look for the quick fix or "magic pill" for increasing maximum sprinting speed. In actuality, the formula is quite simple: make the muscles stronger and more efficient via a sound strength-training regimen combined with improved sprint-technique training. Incorporating different speed modalities into an athlete's training regimen can break the monotony that sometimes sets in even while following a sound program, but be careful not to overuse them. Prioritizing and individualizing are critical in today's sports environment. Increased competition and focus on winning, coupled with less time to achieve the necessary level of fitness provides a daunting challenge to coaches and athletes alike. Devising a systematic, disciplined approach is a must. The drills in the following chapters should be used to maximize speed with this in mind.

Standing Stationary Arm Swings
Arm Action

Purpose
Improve running mechanics and speed by providing teaching cues for upper-body movement while in a stationary position

Procedure

- Stand with the feet together and swing the arms in a sprinting motion.
- Each arm should move as one piece with the elbow bent at about 90 degrees.
- Keep the hands relaxed.
- The hands should come up to about shoulder level in front of the body and should pass the gluteus in the back.
- The arm action should be forward and back without crossing the midline of the body.

Complex Variations

- Seated Arm Swings: Sit on the floor with your legs straight out in front of you and swing the arms as described above. Be careful not to bounce off of the floor as the drill becomes more vigorous. This drill will help train the correct position of the arms as the hands pass the lowest point of the swing by avoiding contact with the ground.
- Weighted Arm Swings: Use light dumbbells held in the hands to work on shoulder strength. Use enough resistance to provide a good training stimulus but not so much as to alter good arm mechanics.
- Contrast-Resisted Arm Swings: Perform arm swings with 1- to 2-pound weights for 10 to 20 arm swings, then drop the weights and perform 10 to 20 arm swings without resistance.

2

Ankling
Basic-Technique Speed

Purpose
Increase foot speed and elastic ankle strength

Procedure
- Jog with very short steps, emphasizing the plantar flexion phase of ground contact and low foot recovery.
- Keep quiet but fast feet.
- Land and push off the ball of the foot. Minimize ground contact and maximize foot contacts.

Straight-Leg Shuffle

Basic-Technique Speed

Purpose

Increase hip strength and elastic ankle strength

Procedure

- Run while keeping the legs straight and the foot dorsiflexed.
- Emphasize fast ground contact with the ball of the foot and pulling through with the hips.

4

Butt-Kickers
Basic-Technique Speed

Purpose
Increase foot speed

Procedure
- From a jog, pull the heel of the lower leg up to and bounce off the gluteus.
- As the leg bends, the knee should come forward and up.

Wall Slides

Basic-Technique Speed

Purpose

Improve knee lift and enhance frequency of turnover

Procedure

- Perform these the same way as the Butt-Kickers but do not allow the heel of the recovery leg to travel behind the body.

6

A-March Walk

Supplemental Speed

Purpose

Increase foot speed

Procedure

- March using perfect posture and arm action.
- The knee on the recovery leg should be brought high and stay fully flexed while keeping the ankle close to the gluteus and dorsiflexed.
- When the recovery knee is at the highest point, the opposite "ground" foot should emphasize plantar flexion.

A-Skips
Supplemental Speed

Purpose
Increase hip extension, flexion strength, and ankle-muscle stiffness

Procedure
- Skip with the same mechanics discussed in the A-March Walk.
- While in the air, emphasize the high recovery posture used in the A-March Walk.
- Keep the upper body in an upright and steady position at all times; the foot strike should be quiet but explosive, emphasizing muscle stiffness at the ankle.
- Be careful not to slam the foot onto the ground.

Complex Variations
- A-Form Runs: Perform form runs, emphasizing the pronounced mechanics practiced in the A-Skips.
- Skipping Paw Drill: This is basically the A-Skip drill with an aggressive pawing motion (a quick leg extension followed by an explosive hip extension).

8

B-March Walk

Supplemental Speed

Purpose

Improve hip-extension mechanics and enhance hamstring firing

Procedure

- March as you did in the A-March Walk.
- Allow the recovering leg to extend in front of you after a high-knee raise.
- Paw down and drive the hips through.

B-Skips
Supplemental Speed

Purpose
Increase stride length and frequency; enhance hamstring and hip performance; improve muscle stiffness at the ankle complex

Procedure
- Perform the B leg movement (that is, the recovery leg's knee blocks as high as possible) while skipping.
- Emphasize pawing and drive the hips through.

Complex Variation
- B-Form Runs: Run while using B leg movements.

10

Ladder Speed Run

Agility Ladder (Stick)

Purpose

Enhance timing and stride frequency while teaching quick turnover

Procedure

- Run through an agility ladder (sticks 18 inches, or 46 centimeters, apart) as fast as possible, touching both feet down between each rung.
- Emphasize lifting the knee high and quickly contacting the ground.

Ladder Stride Run

Agility Ladder (Stick)

Purpose

Enhance timing and stride frequency while teaching quick turnover

Procedure

- Run through an agility ladder (sticks 18 inches, or 46 centimeters, apart) as fast as possible, touching one foot down between every other rung.
- Emphasize upright posture with sound arm and leg mechanics.

Speed

12

Single-Leg Run-Through
Hurdle

Purpose
Enhance stride frequency while strengthening hip flexors and improving lower-body ambidexterity

Procedure
- Set 8 to 10 6- to 12-inch (15- to 32-centimeter) hurdles about 3 feet (91 centimeters) apart.
- Run with one leg outside the hurdles and the other going over the hurdles.
- Emphasize a straight outside leg (as in a shuffle) and a quick A motion with the hurdling leg.

Run-Through
Hurdle

Purpose

Enhance stride frequency while strengthening hip flexors and improving lower-body ambidexterity

Procedure

- Set 8 to 10 6- to 12-inch (15- to 32-centimeter) hurdles about 3 feet (91 centimeters) apart.
- Perform an A-Form Run over the hurdles.
- Emphasize quick "knee up/toe up" with a quick heel-to-gluteus recovery.
- Perform the exercise with a two-foot strike between each hurdle (maintaining the same lead leg through the drill), or run faster with a one-foot strike between hurdles.

14

Hurdle Fast Legs
Hurdle

Purpose

Enhance stride frequency while strengthening hip flexors and improving lower-body ambidexterity

Procedure

- Stagger 8 to 10 6- to 12-inch (15- to 32-centimeter) hurdles so that half line up with the right leg and the other half line up with the left leg.
- The hurdle pattern should be a hurdle for the left leg followed by one for the right leg with the hurdles 3 feet (91 centimeters) apart; repeat the pattern.
- The leg sequence entails hurdling the left foot over the left hurdle then taking two steps to the next hurdle for the right foot.

Light Sled/Tire Pulls
Resisted Speed

Purpose
Enhance running strength and power and improve stride length

Procedure
- Attach a weighted sled or car tire to yourself, which you then drag.
- Emphasize proper sprinting mechanics.
- Do not make the sled so heavy that acceleration mechanics are needed to pull it.

16

Uphill Speed Runs
(1- to 3-Degree Incline)
Resisted Speed

Purpose

Enhance running strength and power and improve stride length

Procedure

- Gravity provides resistance on uphill runs; emphasize perfect maximum-speed mechanics.
- Do not exceed a 3-degree incline if the goal is to develop maximum running speed.
- Higher inclines are more appropriate for acceleration mechanics and will be discussed later.

Parachute Running

Resisted Speed

Purpose

Enhance running strength and power and improve stride length

Procedure

- Wear a belt with a small parachute attached by a cord. Have a partner hold the parachute behind you.
- Start running. The parachute deploys in zero to four steps, depending on wind conditions and the parachute model, and provides extra air resistance.

18

Sand Running
Resisted Speed

Purpose

Increase stride length and hip strength

Procedure

- Sprinting on the beach in loose sand makes sprinting more difficult and can provide good resistance training.
- It also provides increased proprioception to the locomotive environment.

19

Contrast Parachute Running
Contrast-Resisted Runs

Purpose

Enhance stride length of start and turnover at top speed; increase starting speed and transition to top speed

Procedure

- Attach a parachute to yourself, which is to be dragged behind you during the run.
- Emphasize proper speed mechanics.
- After a buildup and 10 to 20 yards (9 to 18 meters) of near-maximum running, release the Velcro belt to allow for unresisted running.
- You should feel an "over-speed" sensation over the next 10 to 20 yards (9 to 18 meters).

Uphill-to-Flat Contrast Speed Runs (15- to 20-Degree Incline)
Contrast-Resisted Runs

Purpose

Enhance stride length of start and turnover at top speed; increase starting speed and transition to top speed

Procedure

- Position yourself 10 to 20 yards (9 to 18 meters) below the top of a hill with a 15- to 20-degree incline).
- Quickly build up to near-maximum speed by the time you are 10 to 15 yards (9 to 14 meters) below the top of the hill.
- Continue to increase speed as you go over the hill to flat ground.
- Hit a higher gear as you transition to the flat ground, running an additional 15 to 25 yards (14 to 23 meters) over the flat ground.

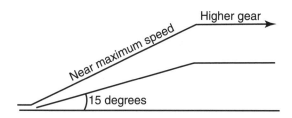

21

Contrast Sled/Tire Pulls

Contrast-Resisted Runs

Purpose

Enhance stride length of start and turnover at top speed; increase starting speed and transition to top speed

Procedure

- Attach a weighted sled or tire to yourself, which you will drag during the run.
- Emphasize proper speed mechanics.
- After a buildup and 10 to 20 yards (9 to 18 meters) of near-maximum running, release the Velcro belt to allow for unresisted running.
- You should feel an "over-speed" sensation over the next 10 to 20 yards (9 to 18 meters).

Downhill Speed Runs
(3- to 7-Degree Decline)

Assisted Speed

Purpose

Increase top-end speed and stride frequency

Procedure

- Gravity provides assistance on downhill runs.
- Emphasize perfect maximum-speed mechanics.
- You can exceed a 3- to 7-degree decline if your goal is to develop maximum running speed, but be aware that overstriding will result in deceleration and interfere with your speed development.
- Perform these drills on a grass surface rather than on asphalt to avoid injury if you fall.

23

Downhill-to-Flat
Contrast Speed Runs
(3- to 5-Degree Decline)
Contrast-Assisted Runs

Purpose

Increase top-end speed and stride frequency

Procedure

- Position yourself 10 to 20 yards (9 to 18 meters) above the bottom of the hill.
- Quickly build up to near-maximum speed by the time you are about 5 yards (4.6 meters) above the bottom of the hill.
- Continue to increase speed as you transition to flat ground.
- Try to maintain "supra-maximal speed" through the transition and on to the flat ground, running for an additional 10 to 15 yards (9 to 14 meters).

Note: The objective of these drills is to try to maintain "supramaximal" speed for 2 to 3 seconds in the absence of assistance.

Wall Drills
(Acceleration Marches)
Basic-Technique Acceleration

Purpose

Enhance muscle stiffness at ankle complex and improve elastic strength of the lower body

Procedure

- Lean against a wall at about a 45- to 60-degree angle with your arms supporting the body.
- Stay on the balls of the feet at all times.
- Bring one knee up, simulating the acceleration position.
- From this position, bring the recovery leg down and the plant leg up.
- You can perform any number of repetitions of this procedure, or you can do it for a given length of time.

25

Falling Starts
Basic-Technique Acceleration

Purpose
Enhance quick leg turnover at start and teach the proper acceleration lean

Procedure
- Stand with the feet together and lean forward until your balance is lost.
- At this point, accelerate at full speed to catch yourself.
- Run 20 to 30 yards (18 to 27 meters).

Moye (Crouched-Variation) Starts

Basic-Technique Acceleration

Purpose

Improve reaction time and starting response; enhance first-step quickness and acceleration mechanics

Procedure

- Moye Starts provide several positions from which to start, including standing, three-point, and four-point starts.

- For a three- or four-point start, assume the desired position with the hands placed on the ground about two foot-lengths in front of the front foot.

- Begin to lean forward and "explode" when the shoulders go beyond the hands.

27

Basic 40-Yard Model
Basic-Technique Acceleration

Purpose

Teach starting, acceleration, and maximum-speed integration; enhance 40-yard (36.6-meter) test performance

Procedure

- For 40-yard (37-meter) sprint times greater than 4.7 seconds, follow this sequence: Visualize the start, inhale, assume the starting position, hold your breath, and begin. Split your arms, drive the back leg, focus on hard leg drives for about 10 yards (9 meters), exhale and inhale, drive tall in an upright posture, at about 20 yards (18 meters) exhale and inhale again, and finish tall.

- For 40-yard (37-meter) sprint times less than 4.7 seconds, follow this sequence: Visualize the start, inhale, assume the starting position, hold your breath, and begin. Split your arms, drive the back leg, focus on hard leg drives for about 15 yards (14 meters), exhale and inhale, drive tall in an upright posture, and finish tall.

Gears

Supplemental Acceleration

Purpose

Improve transition acceleration and enhance ability to change speeds

Procedure

- Space five cones 20 yards (18 meters) apart.
- Vary running intensity between cones, which will teach you to accelerate and shift (transition) between various speeds (or gears).
- For example, run in second gear (half-speed) between cones 1 and 2, third gear (three-quarter speed) between cones 2 and 3, first gear (one-quarter speed) between cones 3 and 4, and fourth gear (full-speed) between cones 4 and 5.
- You can change the order of the gears to any order that you wish.
- You can also use fewer cones for specific transition work or more cones for conditioning work.

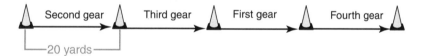

29

Ins and Outs

Supplemental Acceleration

Purpose

Improve transition acceleration and enhance ability to change speeds

Procedure

- Space five cones 15 to 30 yards (14 to 27 meters) apart.
- Start at cone 1.
- Accelerate to submaximal speed by the time you reach cone 2.
- At cone 3, try to go faster than you have ever attempted to go (try to break your maximum speed record).
- At cone 4, reduce intensity but try to maintain stride frequency.

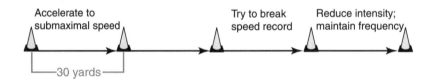

Accelerate to submaximal speed   Try to break speed record   Reduce intensity; maintain frequency

30 yards

Acceleration Runs (17- and 4-Inch)

Acceleration Ladder (Stick)

Purpose

Enhance acceleration and top-end running by teaching proper striding; prevent deceleration due to overstriding

Procedure

- A special ladder is placed on the running surface; sticks may also be used.
- Set up the acceleration ladder rungs, or 18-inch-long (46-centimeter-long) sticks, in the following sequence: 17 inches (43 centimeters) between rungs 1 and 2; add 4 inches (10 centimeters) to this for a full 21 inches (53 centimeters) between rungs 2 and 3; add another 4 inches for 25 inches (64 centimeters) between rungs 3 and 4; and so on.
- Each pair of rungs is placed 4 inches farther apart than the previous distance between rungs, up to your maximum desired stride length.
- As you accelerate you are paced by the rungs.
- This drill promotes proper foot placement and prevents overstriding.

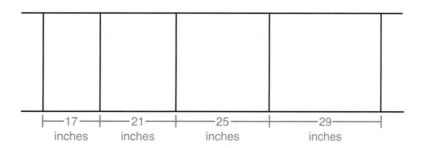

31

Weighted Starts
Resisted Acceleration

Purpose
Enhance elastic strength at start

Procedure
• Using a weighted vest or shot belt will enhance the neural reflex of any start.

Note: This section will focus on pure locomotive acceleration. Chapter 5 will focus on transitional acceleration, involving body-position changes. Unless otherwise indicated, perform this and the following drills over a 10- to 20-yard (9- to 18-meter) distance.

Stadium Stairs

Resisted Acceleration

Purpose

Enhance starting power and stride length

Procedure

- Run up stadium stairs or bleachers for 4 to 8 seconds.

33

Uphill Acceleration Run
Resisted Acceleration

Purpose
Enhance starting power and improve stride length during acceleration

Procedure
- Use a hill with an incline of 20 to 35 degrees.
- Take 4- to 8-second runs up the hill.
- Count your strides and mark your spot at your chosen time.
- Try to beat the distance with fewer strides in subsequent timed runs.

Heavy Sled Pulls

Resisted Acceleration

Purpose

Enhance starting power and stride length

Procedure

- Attach a weighted sled to yourself, which you then drag during a 15- to 20-yard (14- to 18-meter) acceleration run.
- Emphasize an explosive start and acceleration mechanics.

35

Partner-Resisted Starts
Resisted Acceleration

Purpose
Enhance starting power and stride length

Procedure
- You can be resisted during the first 8 to 10 strides by a partner.
- Your partner is situated in front of you with his or her hands on your shoulders; or he or she works from the back, using his or her hands or a towel around your waist to resist the start and acceleration phase.
- The drill ends after 8 to 10 strides.

Partner Tubing-Assisted Acceleration Drill

Assisted Acceleration

Purpose

Improve quick leg recovery in first few steps; enhance stride frequency during acceleration

Procedure

- You and your partner are attached at the waist by a 10- to 20-yard (9- to 18-meter) piece of rubber tubing.
- Your partner lines up at a distance 15 to 25 yards (14 to 23 yards) from you, the assisted athlete.
- Get into the ready position of your choice and, at the signal to begin, explode for 10 to 20 yards (9 to 18 meters) with the aid of the rubber tubing.
- For longer acceleration runs, your partner can run at the signal to begin to provide continued assistance for a longer duration.

37

Harness Pull
Assisted Acceleration

Purpose
Increase acceleration

Procedure
- You and a partner are connected by a harness and handle system that allows you to be towed while your partner runs at half your speed.
- You, the towed athlete, run faster than under normal conditions.

Partner-Assisted Let-Gos

Contrast Acceleration

Purpose

Teach quick transitions in speed and enhance stride frequency of acceleration

Procedure

- Have a partner use his or her hands, a towel, or rope to hold you at about a 45-degree forward lean.
- Start running, pumping the legs and arms explosively.
- Have your partner let you go after about five strides.
- Feel yourself explode out of the falling position, using fast leg and arm movements to recover from the falling sensation.

39

Bullet Belt

Contrast Acceleration

Purpose

Teach quick transitions in speed and enhance stride frequency of acceleration

Procedure

- A bullet belt allows you to be held by a partner while you are attempting to accelerate until enough force is applied to the belt so that the Velcro strip holding it to you breaks.

- There are several techniques used to release the accelerating athlete, including the rip and the pop methods.

Skip for Height
Plyometrics

Purpose

Increase hip extension and flexion strength; improve ankle-muscle stiffness; enhance leg power and stride length

Procedure

- Skip, driving the free knee upward as aggressively as possible.
- Make the arm action very aggressive as well.
- Try to skip as high as possible on each jump.

41

Skip for Distance
Plyometrics

Purpose
Increase hip power and stride length

Procedure
- Skip, driving the knee upward and forward as aggressively as possible.
- Make the arm action equally as aggressive.
- Try to skip as high as possible.

Split-Squat Jumps
Plyometrics

Purpose
Increase hip power and stride length

Procedure
- Start in a lunge position.
- Jump straight into the air and return to the original position.
- Repeat without pausing.
- The knee closest to the ground should never touch the ground.
- Your hands are either placed on either side of your head (near the ears) or may be used in unison to drive upward with each jump.
- Repeat for the other leg.

Complex Variation
- Alternating Split-Squat Jumps: On each jump, the legs switch positions and the other leg is in front of you at ground contact.

43

Bounding
Plyometrics

Purpose

Increase hip extension and flexion strength; improve ankle-muscle stiffness; enhance leg power and stride length

Procedure

- Run, driving the free knee so that the thigh reaches a parallel position with the ground; jump a little on each step.
- This should look like a bouncy run with longer than normal strides.
- Be careful not to reach forward at ground contact.

Single-Leg Bounds
Plyometrics

Purpose

Increase hip extension and flexion strength; improve ankle-muscle stiffness; enhance leg power and stride length

Procedure

- Get a slow running start and begin hopping on a single leg.
- Work on recovery mechanics similar to sprint mechanics (heel to gluteus, high knee, pawing action as the leg prepares to jump again).
- You can measure improvement by comparing the distance covered in a given number of hops over different sets.

45

High Knees
Plyometrics

Purpose
Develop the "thigh-parallel-to-the-ground" technique

Procedure
- Lift knees high into the air in a high marching stance while coming off the ground with the feet.
- Care should be taken to incorporate Butt-Kickers (page 26) when lifting the knee.
- When done correctly, the two parts of the drill should begin to look the same.

Complex Variation
- Backward Knees Drill: This is simply another way to challenge the central nervous system to improve sprint technique.

4 × 4s
Plyometrics

Purpose

Increase hip flexor range of motion and stride length

Procedure

- Continuously alternate between High Knees and Butt-Kickers.
- Perform each four times over 33 yards (30 meters).

47

Heel and Toe Walks
Gait Strength

Purpose

Heel Walks develop the anterior tibialis, train the correct dorsiflexed position of the foot, and help prevent shin splints; Toe Walks develop calf strength and help prevent shin splints

Procedure

- Walk on the heels while keeping the toes off the ground.
- Then walk on the toes while keeping the heels off the ground.

Galloping
Gait Strength

Purpose

Promotes good hip projection and back leg push-off; improves lead-leg mechanics and proper pawing, or leg-cycle, mechanics

Procedure

- Gallop, keeping the trailing ankle locked to emphasize a "spring-loaded" landing and take-off.

49

Pool Drills
Resistance Exercises

Purpose
Good for recovery (hydrostatic pressure helps clear the body of sprinting byproducts—lactate and hydrogen ions) and when injured

Procedure
- Almost any drill can be performed in chest-high water, which adds resistance and reduces impact forces due to buoyancy.

Complex Variation
- Shallow-Water Running: Running in water 1 to 2 feet (31 to 61 centimeters) deep creates resistance and forces high knee lift.

50

Pit Smashers
Acceleration

Purpose
Develop the idea of driving out of the blocks aggressively and powerfully at a low angle; promote full hip, knee, and ankle extension

Procedure
- Drive out of the blocks into a high-jump pit placed about 4 feet (1.2 meters) from the starting line.
- The upper body should slide onto the top of the pit, while the lead knee hits the side of the pit.

Complex Variation
- You can also perform this drill with a sand (long-jump) pit.

Chapter 4

© Bruce Leighty

Agility and Balance Training

John Graham and Vance Ferrigno

Agility and balance are key factors in any athletic endeavor. The constant need to change directions in most sports requires the athlete to maintain a good posture over his or her base of support in order to remain upright. This can be very difficult, for example, when making a lateral cut at very high speed. The following information will discuss how agility and balance can be improved through the judicious use of specific drills.

Developing Agility

Agility generally refers to two sorts of motor functions. On the one hand, it is integral to the ability to explosively start, decelerate, change direction, and accelerate again quickly while maintaining body control and minimizing loss of speed (Costello and Kreis 1993). Agility, in this respect, is important in sport because movements are often initiated from various body positions. So athletes need to be able to react with strength, explosiveness, and quickness from these different positions in short bursts of 10 yards (9 meters) or less before a change of direction is required. On the other hand, agility refers to the ability to coordinate several sport-specific tasks simultaneously, such as when a player dribbles a basketball around a full-court press while looking for an open teammate to whom he or she can pass the ball (Cissik and Barnes 2004). Studies show that agility in these tasks is the primary determining factor to predict success in a sport (Halberg 2001).

Many athletes and coaches believe that agility is primarily determined by genetics and is therefore difficult to improve to any significant degree. Coaches often become enamored with an athlete who possesses natural physical attributes—physical size, strength, vertical and horizontal power, ideal body composition, and so on—that are associated with successful performance. However, these attributes alone will not guarantee success in sports that require agility.

Unfortunately, because of the focus placed on physical attributes, off-season programs often revolve around strength training and conditioning. Agility and speed development at sport-specific speeds is neglected or is emphasized only during small blocks of time during the preseason. In reality, agility involves important neural adaptations that can be developed only over time with many repetitions (Halberg 2001). It takes athletes weeks and months to see improvements in speed and agility. Thus, agility training should be regarded as an integral component of the annual training program. The motor abilities and sport-specific movements that must take place at high speeds during competition have little time to be improved if they are not addressed throughout the off-season. For there is a direct correlation between increased agility and the development of athletic timing, rhythm, and movement (Costello and Kreis 1993).

Considerable research regarding the physical conditioning of athletes has led to a number of changes to how they are taught, coached, and trained. Among these changes is a newfound focus on how agility training is planned and implemented, which has led to the evolution of faster, stronger, and better-conditioned athletes (Costello and Kreis 1993). The key to improving agility is to minimize the loss of speed when shifting the body's center of gravity. Drills that require rapid changes of forward, backward, vertical, and lateral direction help you increase agility and coordination by training the body to make these shifts more quickly and efficiently (Brittenham 1996; Plisk 2000). The following discussion provides a fuller explanation of how agility training yields these benefits:

• Neuromuscular adaptation. Agility training may be the most effective way to address the neuromuscular demands that must be met to effectively perform sport-specific skills, since it often most closely resembles actual sporting activity (Cissik and Barnes 2004). It most closely resembles the intensity, duration, and recovery time found in competition. Including agility training in an annual training cycle is therefore critical to translating overall work on strength and conditioning into gains in the athletic arena.

- Improved athleticism. The primary effect of agility training is increased body control, which results from concentrated kinesthetic awareness. In other words, it focuses on the intricacies of controlling small motor transitions in neck, shoulder, back, hip, knee, and ankle joints to achieve the best possible postural alignment. This enhances the athlete's sense of control, allowing him or her to move faster. In this respect, agility training can also prove crucial to building the confidence of athletes who are frustrated with their performance, in particular for those who have little coordination. It helps such athletes to learn more about themselves.

Creating Agility Programs

When designing an agility program for athletic performance enhancement, a strength and conditioning coach should incorporate forms of training that emphasize these components: strength, power, acceleration, deceleration, coordination, and balance (Cissik and Barnes 2004; Halberg 2001).

Strength   Strength refers to the maximal force that a specific muscle or muscle group can generate at a specified velocity (Harman 2000; Murphy and Forney 1997). When an athlete is in contact with an opponent, the combination of the force applied on him or her by an opponent and his or her own body weight together act as resistance (Cissik and Barnes 2004). Research has demonstrated a strong correlation between lower-body strength and agility. The more emphasis placed on strength and power within a given sporting activity, the greater the need for strength training.

Power   Power may well be the single most important aspect of training. It refers to the rate at which work is done (force × velocity). The faster an athlete gets from one point to another, the greater his or her power. So it can be increased by improving speed.

Acceleration   Acceleration is measured by the change in velocity per unit of time. It plays a central role in going from a stationary position to top speed and then quickly increasing speed again on making a directional change. Having the ability to accelerate quickly could certainly mean the difference between, for example, a running back getting through a hole in the line or being tackled.

Deceleration   Deceleration, for our purposes, refers to the ability to decrease speed or come to a stop from a maximal or near-maximal speed. It is key to slowing the body down to a speed at which one can change direction quickly and then reaccelerate. Deceleration can occur in a number of ways, from slowing within one or more footfalls, to backpedaling, shuffling, or using a crossover step. In all of these situations, it involves eccentric muscle actions. It places a good deal of stress on the joints and is a main source of injury among athletes.

Coordination   Coordination involves the ability to control and process multiple muscle movements in order to effectively perform athletic skills (Cissik and Barnes 2004). It entails the smooth interplay of different muscle groups. Nearly all human movement occurs through multiple joints and muscles working in a coordinated fashion in order to accomplish a given task.

Dynamic balance   Dynamic balance is the ability to maintain control over the body while in motion. When the body is in motion, we gain feedback through the use of sight, kinesthetic awareness, and perturbations made by the nervous system that allow us to adjust our center of gravity (Cissik and Barnes 2004). Agility is closely aligned with balance in that it requires athletes to regulate shifts in the body's center of gravity while undergoing postural deviation (Brittenham 1996). This will be discussed in greater detail later in the chapter.

In addition to understanding the components of a comprehensive agility program, it's also necessary to understand a number of training design variables that need to be considered when developing any sort of training regimen. A brief description of each of these variables is listed below:

- Training factors: Factors such as medical history, age, level of physical maturity, sport-specific skill level, training experience, present fitness level, and plyometric and strength training experience all play a critical role in designing a personalized training program.
- Sequence: Drills that are highly technical, require the highest power output, or are most similar to the demands of the sport played by the athlete should be performed first.
- Repetition: The execution of one complete movement skill.
- Set: A group of agility drills and relief intervals.
- Duration: The distance or time of a work interval.
- Intensity: The speed at which the drill is performed; if the drill is timed, the intensity can be measured by the distance covered.
- Recovery: The period or rest between repetitions; it should be based on the complexity of the skill and the metabolic demands of the sport.
- Volume load: The quantity of exercise performed per workout; for example, an athlete may perform four drills on an agility ladder, doing each drill twice.
- Frequency: The number of training sessions performed in a given week; athletes should perform an agility-training workout twice per week during the off-season and once per week during the season.
- Drill selection: This is based mainly on four factors—the movement patterns of the sport, the time and distance of prescribed work intervals, how long the subsequent rest intervals are (this will vary according to training objectives), and drill complexity (Cissik and Barnes 2004).
- Equipment: Once the athlete is able to demonstrate proper technique at sport-specific speeds, the introduction of other athletes in the field of play as partners or opponents, as well as implements like exercise balls, resistance bands, and sport cords, can be employed to increase the complexity of drills. Suggestions for how to increase complexity are included in the drill section of this chapter.

Perfecting Agility Techniques

When instructing athletes on the execution of agility exercises, it is critical to discuss technique. Visual focus, arm action, and recovery all play a valuable role in performing agility drills correctly. Let's look at each of these factors in turn:

- Visual focus: The athlete's head should be in a neutral position with the eyes focused directly ahead, regardless of the direction of movement or pattern called for in the drill. Exceptions to this guideline arise when the athlete is required to focus on another athlete or an object. Additionally, getting the head around and finding a new focus point should initiate all directional changes and transitions (Cissik and Barnes 2004).

- Arm action: Powerful arm movement during transitional and directional changes is essential in order to reacquire a high rate of speed. Inadequate or improper arm movement may result in a loss of speed or efficiency.

- Recovery: Drills should be performed at work and rest intervals consistent with the sport for which the athlete is training.

Balance Training

Although agility is very important for the athlete in sporting activities, it does not stand alone. Since agility fundamentally involves high-speed changes of direction, it follows that the body must be kept in balance to avoid falling over. As briefly mentioned earlier, balance training therefore prepares athletes to perform when their center of mass moves outside their base of support, such as when making a sharp lateral turn.

In movement there is a constant interplay of losing and regaining our balance that ultimately propels us in the direction we want to move. The human body moves in three planes of motion: the sagittal plane, the frontal plane, and the transverse (or rotational) plane. In everything we do, we constantly have to overcome the forces of gravity, ground reaction, and momentum in each of these planes. This endless cycle of reducing and producing force is all held together by balance.

In this section we'll consider the following key issues: the function of the nervous system with regard to balance, the role strength plays in balance, and the use of balance devices (sometimes referred to as environment enhancers)—whose effectiveness we will examine.

Controlling Balance

Balance is maintained as a result of the interaction of three systems: the visual, the vestibular, and the proprioceptive systems.

Vision plays a significant role in balance. Your eyes give you a picture of the world and where you are in relation to other things in it. Approximately 20 percent of the nerve fibers in the eyes interact with the vestibular system.

The vestibular apparatus, an organ located in the inner ear, is responsible for maintaining general equilibrium. The receptors contained within the vestibular apparatus are sensitive to any changes in head position or movement direction. These receptors provide information regarding linear acceleration (being able to sense forward and backward, as well as upward and downward, movement) and angular acceleration, which enables you to detect rotation of the head while keeping the eyes still. The vestibular apparatus exerts direct control over the eyes so they can directly compensate for head movements. This is crucial in sports where tracking moving objects or an opponent with head and eye movement is a constant necessity. With head movement, receptors in the vestibular apparatus transmit neural information to the cerebellum and the vestibular nuclei located in the brain stem. When the brain receives the message, often reinforced by visual feedback, it sends a signal to the muscles; this tells them to react to the loss of balance. Even standing still is an exercise in dynamic equilibrium. A person is swaying very slightly all the time to all four sides, and balance is maintained by alternate contraction and relaxation of the leg muscles.

The proprioceptive system includes both muscle and joint proprioceptors. Muscle proprioceptors include muscle spindles (which detect changes in muscle length) and Golgi-tendon organs (which detect changes in muscle tension). The joint receptors include free nerve endings, pacinian corpuscles, and Golgi-type receptors. They are responsible for detecting changes in joint angle and pressure that compress and distort the joint capsule. Information from these receptors is relayed to the central nervous system, which then facilitates neuromuscular coordination to provide stability and maintenance of balance.

Assessing Balance

It is important to understand the role of two key factors when assessing balance: dynamic flexibility and strength. With respect to flexibility, it's important to consider the athlete's range of motion in the parts of his or her body that are being tested in order to properly load the muscles to allow balance to take place. For example, if an athlete performs a single-leg forward reach in the sagittal plane and at a certain point in the movement he or she loses balance and has to step out of it, it may be assumed that he or she does not have good balance in the sagittal plane. However, if you look closely at the athlete's ankle joint, you may find that it lacks the proper amount of dorsiflexion to allow the balance reach to take place. It is this, then, that limits his or her ability to perform the movement.

Strength can also limit dynamic balance. If the muscles do not have the strength to eccentrically decelerate a motion, the athlete may not be able to control his or her position and thereby regain balance and change direction in a truly agile manner. Let's think, for example, about a tennis player who is running cross-court to play a backhand and who begins to decelerate to set up the return shot. If he or she does not have the strength to control eccentric loading of his or her body to slow movement, or to load the legs, hips, and back in rotation to set up the backhand, he or she will be out of balance and unable to respond with a powerful return shot.

Balance Devices

Balance may be trained while performing most dynamic drills. The action of moving and changing directions will force the athlete to keep his or her body under control. This will usually begin with slow movements and gradually progress to faster movements as balance is increased. Sometimes balance drills are performed on unstable platforms using commercially available devices. When considering using a balance device, the first question that should be asked is how it will enhance ability to accelerate, decelerate, change direction, and so on. In most sports, movement occurs on a stable field of play with body mass being projected beyond the center of balance and then being regirded to move to the next step. If an athlete is standing on a balance device that is wobbling under his or her feet and is trying to maintain static balance, how much crossover would that have to the movements we described above? Will having the ability to stand on a stability ball truly help the athlete's speed, agility, and quickness? If so, what is the risk (in comparison to the reward) of performing such a drill? All balance devices are tools, and like any tool you must first understand how it is going to help you address a specific need. The purpose of balance devices is not to make the whole body so unstable that greater stability cannot be achieved. Instead, they must complement the drills by very subtly introducing controlled instability, which will in time create greater stability overall.

The following section provides drills whose main objective is to enhance agility and balance as part of a wider training plan for speed, agility, and quickness. A general format for implementing each drill is provided, and some include examples or variations. With these guidelines you can create as many varieties as you need.

Carioca

Assorted Biomotor Skills

Purpose

Develop balance, flexibility in the hips, footwork, and lateral speed

Procedure

- Start in a two-point stance.
- Step with right foot over the left leg.
- Move the left foot to the left behind the right leg.
- Step with the right foot behind the left leg.

Crossover Skipping
Assorted Biomotor Skills

Purpose

Develop explosive crossover mechanics for direction changes; enhance explosive contralateral hip flexion and extension

Procedure

- Start in a two-point stance.
- Begin skipping laterally to your left, crossing the right leg over the left.
- Emphasize left-hip extension and right-hip flexion.
- Rotate the hips to the left as the right leg goes over and in front of the left.
- Keep the shoulders square to the front.

20-Yard Shuttle

Line Sprints

Purpose

Improve ability to change direction, footwork, and reaction time

Procedure

- Start in a two-point stance straddling the starting line.
- Turn to the right, sprint, and touch a line 5 yards (4.6 meters) away with your right hand.
- Turn back to the left, sprint 10 yards (9 meters), and touch the far line with your left hand.
- Turn back to the right and sprint 5 yards (4.6 meters) through the start line to the finish.

Complex Variation

- 20-Yard Combination Agility Drill: Perform different biomotor skills on each leg of the line drill.

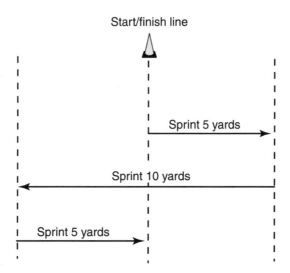

Start/finish line

Sprint 5 yards

Sprint 10 yards

Sprint 5 yards

30-Yard T-Drill
Line Sprints

Purpose

Develop agility, conditioning, and flexibility in abductors and adductors; improve strength

Procedure

- Start in a two-point stance.
- Sprint forward 5 yards (4.6 meters) to a marked spot on the ground.
- Side-shuffle to the right and touch a line 5 yards (4.6 meters) away with the right hand.
- Shuffle back to the left 10 yards (9 meters) and touch the far line with your left hand.
- Shuffle back to the right 5 yards (4.6 meters) to the marked spot.
- Touch the marked spot with either foot and backpedal through the start line to the finish.

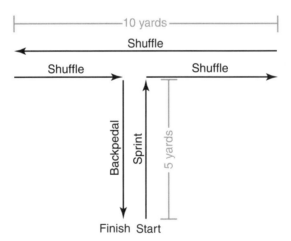

Squirm
Line Sprints

Purpose
Develop footwork and reaction time

Procedure
- Start in a two-point stance.
- Sprint forward 5 yards (4.6 meters).
- Rotate 360 degrees and sprint another 5 yards (4.6 meters).
- Rotate 360 degrees again and sprint another 5 yards (4.6 meters).
- Sprint right or left for 10 yards (9 meters).

Complex Variations
- Put your right hand down on the ground during the first (right) 360-degree rotation and your left hand down on the ground during the second (left) 360-degree rotation.
- Vary the distance.
- Make turns when commanded by your coach.
- Use various biomotor skill combinations throughout the drill.

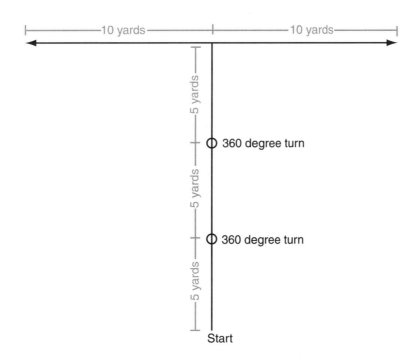

40-Yard Sprint

Line Sprints

Purpose

Develop agility and conditioning

Procedure

- Start in a two-point stance on the starting line.
- Sprint 5 yards (4.6 meters) to the first line, touch the line with your right hand, return to the starting line, and touch it with your left hand.
- Sprint 10 yards (9 meters) to the second line, touch the line with your right hand, return to the starting line, and touch it with your left hand.
- Sprint 5 yards (4.6 meters) to the first line, touch the line with your right hand, and return to the starting line.

Complex Variations

- Combine biomotor skills during each leg of the drill.
- Start the drill from various positions (for example, lying, sitting, and so on).
- Add tumbling to each turn.

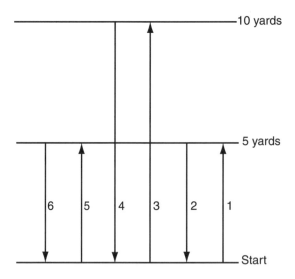

60-Yard Shuttle Sprint

Line Sprints

Purpose

Improve agility and conditioning

Procedure

- Start in a two-point stance.
- Sprint forward 5 yards (4.6 meters) to the first line and touch it with either hand. Turn and return to the start line.
- Sprint forward 10 yards (9 meters) to the second line and touch it with either hand. Turn and return to the start line.
- Sprint forward 15 yards (14 meters) to the third line and touch it with either hand. Turn and return through the start line.

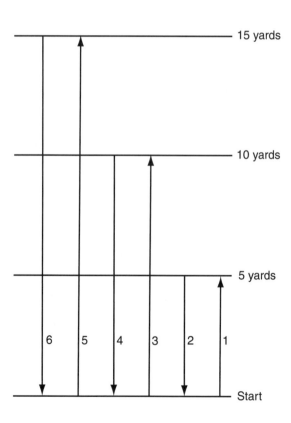

40-Yard Lateral Shuffle

Line Sprints

Purpose

Improve agility, conditioning, and flexibility in abductors and adductors; develop strength

Procedure

- Start in a two-point stance, straddling the start line.
- Shuffle 5 yards (4.6 meters) to the first line, touch it with the right foot, shuffle back to the starting line, and touch it with the left foot.
- Shuffle 10 yards (9 meters) to the second line, touch it the with right foot, shuffle back to the starting line, and touch it with the left foot.
- Shuffle 5 yards (4.6 meters) to the first line, touch it with the right foot, and shuffle back to the starting line.

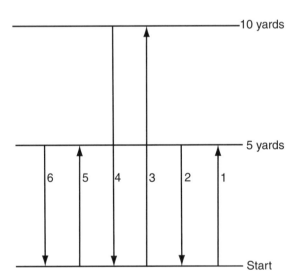

40-Yard Backpedal-Forward

Line Sprints

Purpose

Improve agility, ability to change direction, and conditioning

Procedure

- Start in a two-point stance with your back to the starting line.
- Backpedal 5 yards (4.6 meters) to the first line, touch it with either foot, sprint back to the starting line, and touch it with either foot.
- Backpedal 10 yards (9 meters) to the second line, touch it with either foot, sprint back to the starting line, and touch it with either foot.
- Backpedal 5 yards (4.6 meters) to the first line, touch it with either foot, and sprint back to the starting line.

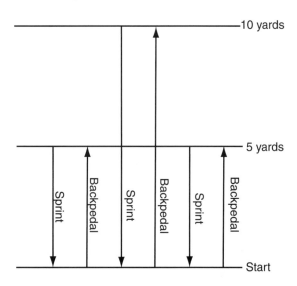

55-Yard Sprint-Backpedal
Line Sprints

Purpose

Develop acceleration and stopping ability

Procedure

- Sprint forward 10 yards (9 meters).
- Backpedal 5 yards (4.6 meters).
- Sprint forward 10 yards.
- Backpedal 5 yards.
- Sprint forward 10 yards.
- Backpedal 5 yards.
- Sprint forward 10 yards.
- Accelerate with 100-percent effort.
- Maximize your forward lean when initially accelerating.
- Minimize your braking distance by quickly dropping your center of gravity.
- Use short, choppy steps to minimize your stopping distance.

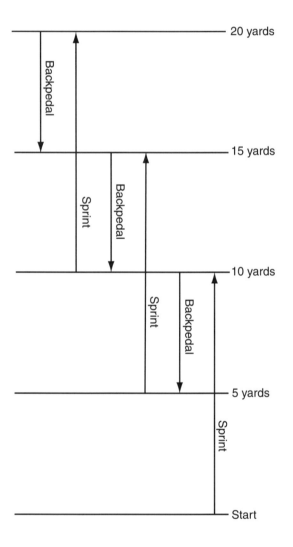

100-Yard Sprint

Line Sprints

Purpose

Improve ability to change direction, footwork, and reaction time

Procedure

- Start in a two-point stance on the starting line.
- Sprint 5 yards (4.6 meters) to the first line, touch it with the right hand, return to the starting line, and touch it with the left hand.
- Sprint 10 yards (9 meters) to the second line, touch it with the right hand, return to the starting line, and touch it with the left hand.
- Sprint 15 yards (14 meters) to the first line, touch it with the right hand, return to the starting line, and touch it with the left hand.
- Sprint 20 yards (18 meters) to the second line, touch it with the right hand, return to the starting line, and touch it with the left hand.

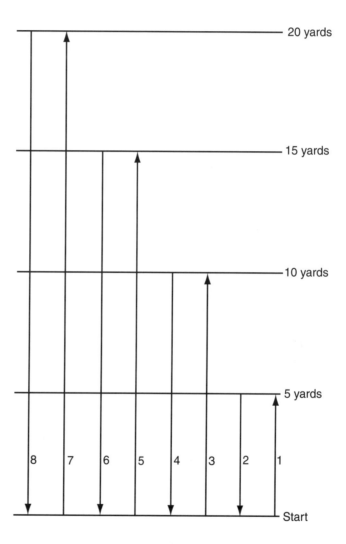

40-Yard Square—Carioca

Cone Drill

Purpose

Improve ability to change direction, flexibility in hips, and footwork

Procedure

- Place a cone at each corner of the square.
- Start in a two-point stance.
- Begin on the right side of the square and sprint forward 10 yards (9 meters).
- At the first cone make a reverse pivot.
- Carioca 10 yards (9 meters) to the next cone.
- Reverse pivot and backpedal 10 yards (9 meters) to the next cone.
- Reverse pivot and carioca 10 yards (9 meters) to the finish.

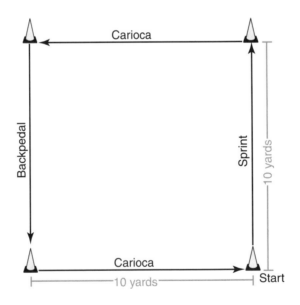

15-Yard Turn Drill
Cone Drill

Purpose

Improve ability to change direction, flexibility in hips, and footwork

Procedure

- Start in a two-point stance.
- Sprint forward 5 yards (4.6 meters) to cone 1 and make a sharp right turn around it.
- Sprint to cone 2, located 5 yards (4.6 meters) to the right of the start and diagonal from the first cone, and make a left turn around it.
- Sprint 5 yards (4.6 meters) through the finish.

Complex Variations

- Put the inside hand on the ground when making turns.
- Change the distance to the cones.
- Make turns on command, not at the cones.

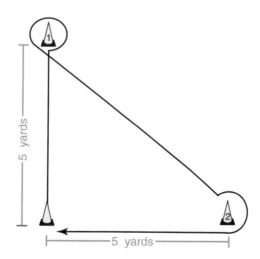

20-Yard Square
Cone Drill

Purpose

Improve ability to change direction, body position, transitions between skills, and cutting

Procedure

- Start in a two-point stance.
- Sprint 5 yards (4.6 meters) to cone 1 and make sharp right cut.
- Shuffle right 5 yards (4.6 meters) and make a sharp cut back at cone 3.
- Backpedal 5 yards (4.6 meters) to cone 4 and make a sharp left cut.
- Left-shuffle to cone 1.

Complex Variations

- Start from different positions (for example, lying, a four-point stance, and so on).
- Change the distance of the cones to match the demands of your sport.
- Change the skills employed during each leg to meet your specific needs.
- Cut with the inside or outside leg.
- Cut on the outside of the cone or circle around the cones.
- Put the inside hand on the ground during turns.

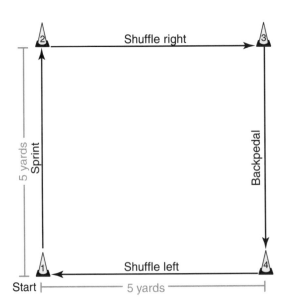

X-Pattern Multiskill
Cone Drill

Purpose
Improve transitional movement and cutting ability

Procedure
- Start in a two-point stance.
- Sprint 10 yards (9 meters) to cone 1.
- At cone 1, sprint diagonally 14 yards (13 meters) to cone 2.
- Backpedal 10 yards (9 meters) to cone 3.
- At cone 3, sprint diagonally 14 yards (13 meters) to cone 4.

Complex Variations
- Start from different positions (for example, lying, a four-point stance, and so on).
- Change the distance of the cones to match the demands of your sport.
- Change skills employed during each leg to meet your specific needs.
- Cut with the inside or outside leg.
- Cut on the outside of the cone or circle around the cones.
- Put the inside hand on the ground during turns.

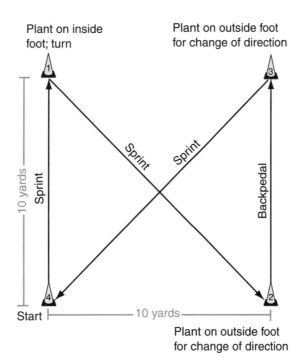

Figure Eights
Cone Drill

Purpose
Improve ability to change direction and reaction time

Procedure
- Position two flat cones 5 to 10 yards (4.6 to 9 meters) apart.
- Start in a two-point stance.
- Run a figure eight between the cones, placing your inside hand on each cone while you make the turn.

Complex Variations
- Change the distance between the cones.
- Change the radius of the turns.
- Start the drill from various positions (for example, lying, sitting, a four-point stance, and so on).

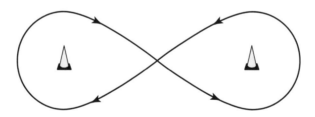

Z-Pattern Run

Cone Drill

Purpose

Improve transitional movement and turning ability

Procedure

- Position three cones on two lines 5 yards (4.6 meters) apart such that the cones on line 1 are at 0, 10, and 20 yards (0, 9, and 18 meters), and the cones on line 2 are at 5, 15, and 25 yards (4.6, 14, and 23 meters).
- Start in a two-point stance.
- Sprint diagonally 5 yards (4.6 meters) to the closest cone, plant the outside foot, and run around the cone.
- Continue to sprint diagonally to, and run around, each cone.

Complex Variations

- Start from different positions (for example, lying, a four-point stance, and so on).
- Change the distance of the cones to match the demands of your sport.
- Change the skills employed during each leg to meet your specific needs.
- Cut with the inside or outside leg.
- Put the inside hand on the ground during turns.

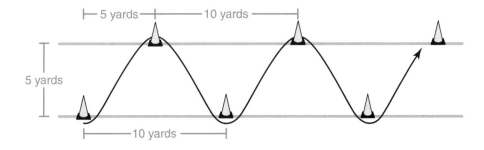

Agility

Zigzag

Cone Drill

Purpose

Improve footwork and quickness

Procedure

- Start in a two-point stance.
- Stand facing a row of 10 cones, each cone 1 yard (.9 meter) apart.
- Quickly step forward and diagonally with the right foot to the right of the first cone and then slide the left foot next to the right foot.
- Lead with the left foot to the left side of the next cone and then slide the right foot up to the left foot.
- Zigzag through all the cones quickly and explosively.

Z-Pattern Cuts

Cone Drill

Purpose

Improve cutting ability

Procedure

- Place cones as indicated in the figure.
- Start in a two-point stance.
- Sprint to cone 1, plant on the outside leg, and cut sharply toward cone 2.

Complex Variations

- Start from different positions (for example, lying, a four-point stance, and so on).
- Change the distance of the cones to match the demands of your sport.
- Change the skills employed during each leg to meet specific needs.
- Cut with the inside or outside leg.
- Cut on the outside of the cone or circle around the cones.
- Put the inside hand on the ground during turns.

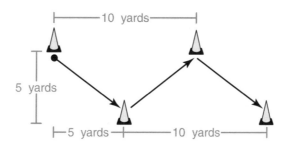

40-Yard Square Drill—Sprint, Bear Crawl, Backpedal

Cone Drill

Purpose

Improve ability to change direction, body position, transitions between skills, and cutting ability

Procedure

- Position four cones in a square 10 yards (9 meters) apart such that cone 1 is on the start line, cone 2 is 10 yards (9 meters) straight ahead, cone 3 is 10 yards (9 meters) to the left of cone 2, and cone 4 is 10 yards (9 meters) to the left of cone 1.
- Start in a ready position at cone 1.
- Make two consecutive trips around the square, one counterclockwise and one clockwise.
- On a signal to begin, sprint forward from cone 1 to cone 2.
- Upon reaching cone 2, bear crawl to the left while facing out until you reach cone 3.
- Backpedal from cone 3 to cone 4.
- Bear crawl to the right from cone 4 to cone 1.
- Upon reaching the starting point, repeat the drill going in the opposite direction.

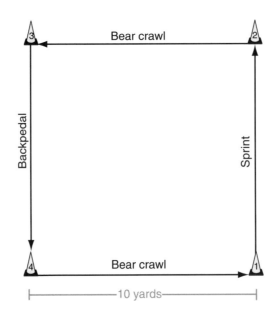

40-Yard Square Drill—Sprint, Single-Leg Hop, Backpedal
Cone Drill

Purpose

Improve ability to change direction, body position, transitions between skills, and cutting ability

Procedure

- Position four cones in a square 10 yards (9 meters) apart such that cone 1 is on the start line, cone 2 is 10 yards (9 meters) straight ahead, cone 3 is 10 yards (9 meters) to the left of cone 2, and cone 4 is 10 yards (9 meters) to the left of cone 1.
- Start in a ready position at cone 1.
- Make two consecutive trips around the square, one counterclockwise and one clockwise.
- On a signal to begin, sprint forward from cone 1 to cone 2.
- Upon reaching cone 2, single-leg hop on the left leg to the left while facing out until you reach cone 3.
- Backpedal from cone 3 to cone 4, single-leg hop on the right leg to the right from cone 4 to cone 1.
- Upon reaching the starting point, repeat the drill going in the opposite direction.

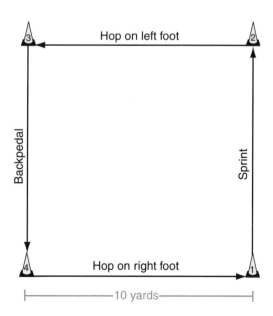

Star Drill—Sprint, Backpedal, Shuffle

Cone Drill

Purpose

Improve ability to change direction, body position, transitions between skills, and cutting ability

Procedure

- Position four cones in a square 10 yards (9 meters) apart such that cone 1 is on the start line, cone 2 is 10 yards (9 meters) straight ahead, cone 3 is 10 yards (9 meters) to the left of cone 2, and cone 4 is 10 yards (9 meters) to the left of cone 1. Position a fifth cone in the middle of the square.

- Start in a ready position at cone 1.

- Sprint diagonally from cone 1 to cone 5.

- Backpedal diagonally from cone 5 to back cone 1.

- Shuffle laterally from cone 1 to cone 4.

- Sprint diagonally from cone 4 to cone 5.

- Backpedal from cone 5 to back cone 4.

- Shuffle laterally from cone 4 to cone 3.

- Sprint diagonally from cone 3 to cone 5.

- Backpedal from cone 5 to back cone 3.

- Shuffle laterally from cone 3 to cone 2.

- Sprint diagonally from cone 2 to cone 5.

- Backpedal from cone 5 to back cone 2.

- Shuffle laterally from cone 2 to cone 1.

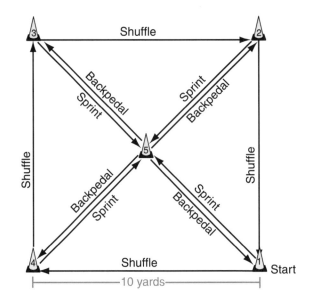

Star Drill—Sprint, Carioca, Backpedal

Cone Drill

Purpose

Improve ability to change direction, body position, transitions between skills, and cutting ability

Procedure

- Position four cones in a square 10 yards (9 meters) apart such that cone 1 is on the start line, cone 2 is 10 yards (9 meters) straight ahead, cone 3 is 10 yards (9 meters) to the left of cone 2, and cone 4 is 10 yards (9 meters) to the left of cone 1. Position a fifth cone in the middle of the square.

- Start in a ready position at cone 1.

- Sprint diagonally from cone 1 to cone 5.

- Carioca diagonally from cone 5 back to cone 1.

- Backpedal from cone 1 to cone 4.

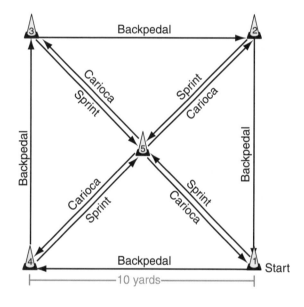

- Sprint diagonally from cone 4 to cone 5.
- Carioca diagonally from cone 5 back to cone 4.
- Backpedal from cone 4 to cone 3.
- Sprint diagonally from cone 3 to cone 5.
- Carioca diagonally from cone 5 back to cone 3.
- Backpedal from cone 3 to cone 2.
- Sprint diagonally from cone 2 to cone 5.
- Carioca diagonally from cone 5 back to cone 2.
- Backpedal from cone 2 to cone 1.

Star Drill—Sprint, Bear Crawl, Shuffle

Cone Drill

Purpose

Improve ability to change direction, body position, transitions between skills, and cutting ability

Procedure

- Position four cones in a square 10 yards (9 meters) apart such that cone 1 is on the start line, cone 2 is 10 yards (9 meters) straight ahead, cone 3 is 10 yards (9 meters) to the left of cone 2, and cone 4 is 10 yards (9 meters) to the left of cone 1. Position a fifth cone in the middle of the square.

- Start in a ready position at cone 1.

- Sprint diagonally from cone 1 to cone 5.

- Bear crawl diagonally from cone 5 back to cone 1.

- Shuffle laterally from cone 1 to cone 4.

- Sprint diagonally from cone 4 to cone 5.

- Bear crawl from cone 5 back to cone 4.

- Shuffle laterally from cone 4 to cone 3.

- Sprint diagonally from cone 3 to cone 5.

- Bear crawl from cone 5 back to cone 3.

- Shuffle laterally from cone 3 to cone 2.

- Sprint diagonally from cone 2 to cone 5.

- Bear crawl from cone 5 back to cone 2.

- Shuffle laterally from cone 2 to cone 1.

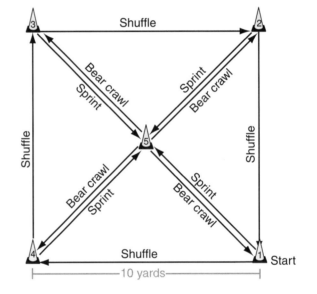

Complex Variation

- Perform the drill replacing shuffles with backpedals.

Five-Cone Snake Drill
Cone Drill

Purpose

Improve ability to change direction, body position, transitions between skills, and cutting ability

Procedure

- Position four cones in a square 10 yards (9 meters) apart such that cone 1 is on the start line, cone 2 is 10 yards (9 meters) straight ahead, cone 3 is 10 yards (9 meters) to the left of cone 2, and cone 4 is 10 yards (9 meters) to the left of cone 1. Position a fifth cone in the middle of the square.
- Start in a ready position between cone 1 and cone 2.
- Sprint forward around cone 2.
- Sprint diagonally and around cone 5.
- Sprint diagonally around cone 3.
- Sprint forward around cone 4.
- Sprint diagonally and around cone 5.
- Sprint diagonally around cone 1.
- Sprint from cone 1 to midway between cone 1 and cone 2.

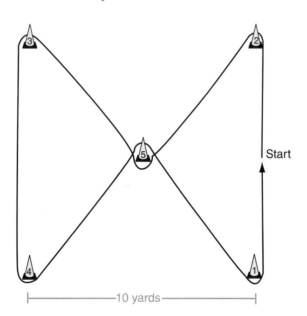

76

S-Drill

Cone Drill

Purpose

Improve ability to change direction, body position, transitions between skills, and cutting ability

Procedure

- Position four cones in an S-shape, such that cone 1 is on a start line, cone 2 is 10 yards (9 meters) forward and 5 yards (4.6 meters) to the right, cone 3 is 10 yards (9 meters) further forward and directly in line with cone 1, and cone 4 is 10 yards (9 meters) further up and in line with cone 2.
- Sprint from cone 1 diagonally and around the outside of cone 2.
- Sprint from cone 2 diagonally and around the outside of cone 3.
- Sprint from cone 3 diagonally and around the outside of cone 4.
- Loop around cone 4 and return in the opposite pattern.

10-Cone Snake Drill
Cone Drill

Agility

Purpose

Improve ability to change direction, body position, transitions between skills, and cutting ability

Procedure

- Place seven cones in a straight line 5 yards (4.6 meters) apart going from left to right. Place three more cones 5 yards (4.6 meters) in front of cones 2, 4, and 6.
- Without crossing your feet, shuffle to the right from cone 1 to cone 2.
- Plant your right foot and drive forward to the cone 5 yards (4.6 meters) in front of cone 2.
- Sprint around the cone and diagonally to cone 3.
- Without crossing your feet, shuffle to the right from cone 3 to cone 4.
- Plant your right foot and drive forward to the cone 5 yards (4.6 meters) in front of cone 4.
- Sprint around the cone and diagonally to cone 5.
- Without crossing your feet, shuffle to the right from cone 5 to cone 6.
- Plant your right foot and drive forward to the cone 5 yards (4.6 meters) in front of cone 6.
- Sprint around the cone and diagonally to cone 7.
- Perform the drill in both directions for one repetition.

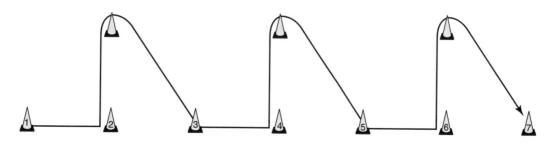

V-Drill
Cone Drill

Purpose

Improve ability to change direction, body position, transitions between skills, and cutting ability

Procedure

- Place three cones to form a 90-degree angle. Cone 1 will be on a starting line. Cones 2 and 3 will be 10 yards (9 meters) to the left and right respectively and 10 yards (9 meters) forward.
- Sprint diagonally forward and to the left to cone 2.
- Plant your left foot and backpedal to cone 1.
- Without pausing, sprint diagonally forward and to the right to cone 3.
- Plant your right foot and backpedal to cone 1.
- A sprint and backpedal in both directions constitute one repetition.

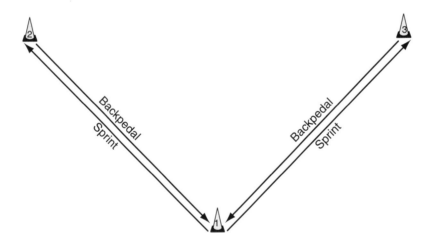

A-Movement

Cone Drill

Purpose

Improve ability to change direction, body position, transitions between skills, and cutting ability

Procedure

- Place five cones in an A-shape such that cone 1 and cone 5 are 10 yards (9 meters) apart on a starting line. Cones 2 and 3 are 5 yards (4.6 meters) in front of cones 1 and 5 and 5 yards (4.6 meters) apart. Cone 4 is 5 yards (4.6 meters) in front of and between cones 2 and 3.
- Sprint from cone 1 to cone 2.
- Shuffle from cone 2 to cone 3.
- Shuffle back from cone 3 to cone 2.
- Sprint from cone 2 to cone 4.
- Backpedal from cone 4 to cone 5.

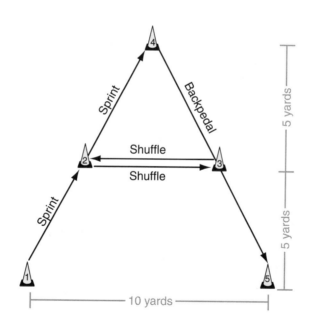

E-Movement
Cone Drill

Purpose

Improve ability to change direction, body position, transitions between skills, and cutting ability

Procedure

- Place six cones in an E-shape such that cone 1 and cone 2 are 10 yards (9 meters) apart on a starting line. Cones 3 and 4 are 5 yards (4.6 meters) in front of cones 1 and 2. Cones 5 and 6 are 5 yards (4.6 meters) in front of cones 3 and 4.
- Shuffle from cone 1 to cone 2.
- Sprint from cone 2 to cone 3.
- Shuffle from cone 3 to cone 4.
- Shuffle back from cone 4 to cone 3.
- Sprint from cone 3 to cone 5.
- Shuffle from cone 5 to cone 6.
- Shuffle back from cone 6 to cone 5.
- Backpedal from cone 5 to cone 2.
- Shuffle from cone 2 to cone 1.

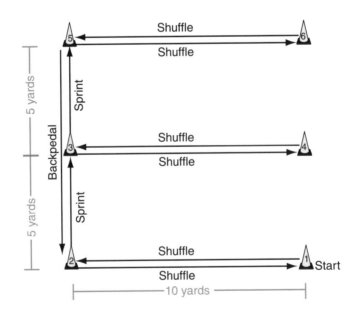

H-Movement

Cone Drill

Purpose

Improve ability to change direction, body position, transitions between skills, and cutting ability

Procedure

- Place six cones in an H-shape such that cone 1 is on a starting line. Cone 2 is 5 yards (4.6 meters) in front of cone 1, and cone 3 is 5 yards (4.6 meters) to the right of cone 2. Cones 4 and 5 are 5 yards (4.6 meters) in front of cones 2 and 3. Cone 6 is 5 yards (4.6 meters) to the right of cone 1.
- Sprint from cone 2 to cone 4.
- Backpedal from cone 4 to cone 2.
- Shuffle from cone 2 to cone 3.
- Sprint from cone 3 to cone 5.
- Backpedal from cone 5 to cone 6.
- Sprint from cone 6 to cone 3.
- Shuffle from cone 3 to cone 2.
- Backpedal from cone 2 to cone 1.

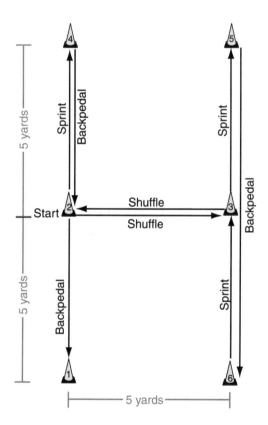

Icky Shuffle

Agility Ladder Drill

Purpose

Enhance coordination and improve lower-body quickness

Procedure

- Start on the left side of the ladder.
- Step laterally with the right foot and place it inside the first square of the ladder, then place the left foot inside the first square.
- Step laterally with the right foot to the right side of the ladder, then advance the left foot to the next square in the ladder.
- Bring the right foot up to the square in which you have your left foot.
- Step laterally to the left side of the ladder and advance the right foot to the next square on the latter.
- Repeat this pattern.

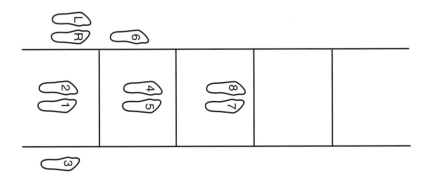

Note: To add complexity to all ladder drills, look up during the drill and avoid looking at your feet. Perform all drills forward and backward.

In-Out Shuffle

Agility Ladder Drill

Purpose

Improve agility, balance, coordination, and quickness

Procedure

- Start in a two-point stance.
- Begin standing sideways to the ladder, with the ladder in front of you.
- Step with the left foot straight ahead into the first square.
- Follow with the right foot into the first square.
- Step back and diagonally with the left foot until it is in front of the second square.
- Follow with the right foot until it is in front of the second square.
- Repeat this sequence throughout the ladder.
- Each foot hits every box.

Complex Variations

- Perform the same pattern with each foot in a separate box.
- Use every other box and increase the length of your lateral step.
- Perform the drill backward (that is, start with the ladder behind you).

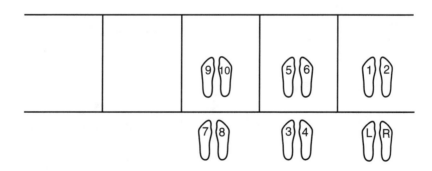

Side Right-In
Agility Ladder Drill

Purpose
Improve agility, balance, coordination, and quickness

Procedure
- Start in a two-point stance.
- Begin standing sideways to the ladder.
- Step with the right foot into the first square.
- Step forward with the left foot over the first square to the other side of the ladder.
- Step laterally with the right foot to the second square.
- Step backward with the left foot, landing in front of the second square.
- Step laterally with the right foot to the third square.
- Repeat this sequence throughout the ladder.

Complex Variation
- Side Left-In: Perform the drill starting with the left foot and use the opposite foot in comparison to the instructions above.

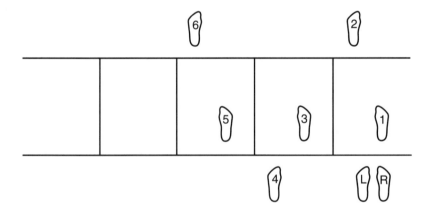

Crossover Shuffle

Agility Ladder Drill

Purpose

Increase flexibility and power in the hips; improve ability to change direction

Procedure

- Stand with the ladder to your right.
- Cross over with the left foot to the first square of the ladder.
- Laterally step with the right foot to the right side of the ladder.
- Immediately cross over with the right foot to the second square of the ladder.
- Laterally step with the left foot to the left side of the ladder.
- Repeat.
- Remember: only one foot is in the ladder at any one time.

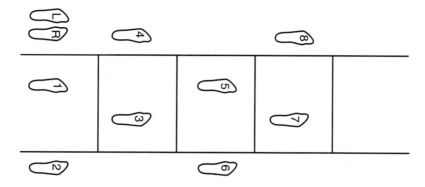

Zigzag Crossover Shuffle
Agility Ladder Drill

Purpose
Improve flexibility in abductors and adductors, footwork, and ability to change direction

Procedure
- Start in a two-point stance.
- Begin on the left side of the agility ladder and perform a crossover step with the left foot in front of the right foot into the first square.
- Bring the right leg behind the left leg to the right side of the first square.

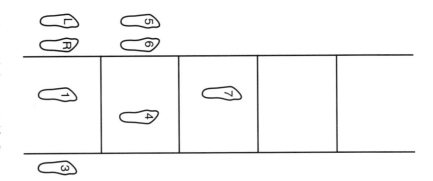

- Laterally step with the left leg to slightly outside the right side of the first square.
- Crossover with the right leg in front of the left to inside the second square.
- Bring the left leg behind the right leg to the left side of the second square.
- Laterally step with the right leg to slightly outside the left side of the second square.
- Continue down the agility ladder in this pattern.

Complex Variation
- Start in a two-point stance on the left side of the ladder, facing backward.
- Perform a crossover step with the right foot in front of the left foot into the first square.
- Bring the left leg behind the right leg to the right side of the first square.
- Step laterally with the right leg in front of the left leg to slightly outside the right side of the first square.
- Cross over with the left leg behind the right leg to inside the second square.
- Bring the right leg in front of the left leg to the left of the second square.
- Step laterally with the left leg to slightly outside the left side.
- Continue down the agility ladder in this pattern.

Snake Jump

Agility Ladder Drill

Purpose

Improve agility, balance, coordination, hip flexibility, and quickness

Procedure

- Start in a two-point stance, straddling one side of the ladder.
- Keeping both feet together, perform a series of quarter-turn jumps.
- The direction the feet should point for each jump is as follows: straight-ahead, right, straight-ahead, left, straight-ahead, and so on.
- This drill forces you to rotate the hips with each jump.

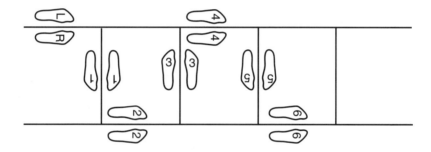

180-Degree Turn
Agility Ladder Drill

Purpose
Improve agility, balance, hip flexibility, and quickness

Procedure
- Start in a two-point stance, straddling the first rung of the ladder.
- Jump and turn 180 degrees with both feet and land straddling the next rung.
- Continue repeating the half-turns into every square through the agility ladder.

Complex Variation
- This drill can be performed facing perpendicular to the ladder.

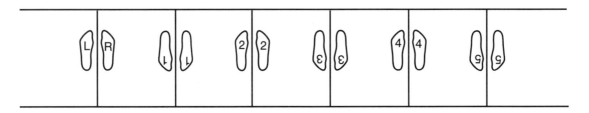

Bag Weave
Bag Drill

Purpose

Improve flexibility, high-knee action, and quickness of foot movements

Procedure

- Start in a two-point stance.
- Starting on the outside of the first of four bags, sprint forward until you are in front of the bag.
- Shuffle the feet to the right until you reach a space between the bags, but do not cross the feet when moving sideways.
- Backpedal quickly until you are one step past the bag.
- Repeat this pattern through all bags until you reach the outside of the last bag. Remember to always keep your shoulders square and to stay in a two-point stance while keeping your head up; use good running form while moving as fast as possible.

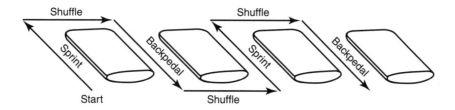

Combo Sidestep/Forward-Back
Bag Drill

Purpose

Improve ability to change direction, flexibility, high-knee action, and quickness of foot movements

Procedure

- Start in a two-point stance with the hands and arms away from the body.
- Sprint laterally over bags 1 and 2.
- Sprint 5 yards (4.6 meters) to the front of bag 3 and shuffle.
- Backpedal 5 yards (4.6 meters) and laterally step over bags 4 and 5.
- Sprint 5 yards (4.6 meters) to the front of bag 6 and shuffle.
- Backpedal 5 yards (4.6 meters) and laterally step over bag 7.

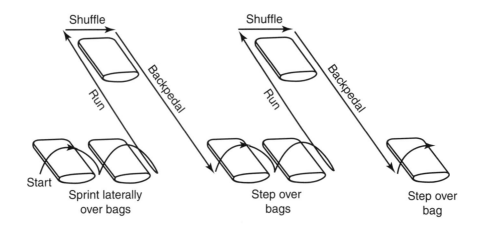

Lateral Weave
Bag Drill

Purpose
Improve quickness of foot movements and reaction time

Procedure
- Start in a two-point stance with the hands and arms away from the body.
- Sidestep laterally over three or four bags quickly to the right or left.
- After crossing the last bag, immediately reverse directions.
- Once you cross the last bag, sprint forward 5 yards (4.6 meters).

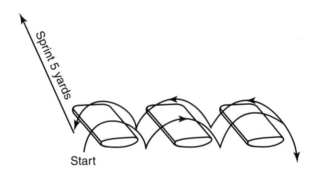

92

Bag Hops
With 180-Degree Turn
Bag Drill

Purpose

Improve quick foot movement and hip flexibility while providing plyometric training

Procedure

- Start in a two-point stance.
- Hop laterally over bag 1, rotating 180 degrees while in the air.
- Land between bags 1 and 2 and immediately hop over bag 2, rotating 180 degrees in the opposite direction.
- Hop and rotate over four to six bags.

93

Wheel
Bag Drill

Purpose

Improve balance and quickness of foot movements

Procedure

- Arrange four bags in an X format.
- With both hands in the middle of the X formed by the bags, stand between two of the bags.
- Start by sidestepping over each bag while rotating around all four bags; keep your hands in contact with the X until you are back at the original starting position.
- Quickly reverse directions and rotate back, sidestepping quickly over all four bags.
- Finish the drill by quickly sprinting 5 yards (4.6 meters) straight ahead out of the bags.

Side-to-Side Skiers
Angle-Board Drill

Purpose
Develop agility and rotational change of direction

Procedure
- Start in a two-point stance on the run.
- Stand perpendicular to the angles in the middle of the run.
- Jump and rotate in midair so as to land with both feet on the right angle and facing the direction from which you have run. Immediately jump back, rotating in midair, to land in the original position.
- Jump and rotate in midair so as to land with both feet on the left angle and facing the direction from which you have run. Immediately jump back, rotating in midair, to land in the original position.
- Repeat.

Agility

Side-to-Side Skiers With Front Rotation

Slide-Board Drill

Purpose

Improve lateral agility, rotational transition, and balance

Procedure

- Start in a two-point stance with a slight bend in the knees.
- Drop into a slight squat.
- Push off the slide board's side support and glide to the opposite side.
- While in transition, rotate counterclockwise so as to land on the opposite support with the push-off foot.
- When you make contact, push off again and repeat.
- Perform this drill to both the right and the left side.

Complex Variations

- Side-to-Side Skiers With Back Rotation: Perform the drill by starting out facing the opposite direction in order to achieve back rotation.
- Combine the front and back rotation versions by doing them one after the other; do the front rotation version and then as soon as you reach the opposite support push off toward the other side, rotating in transition.

Forward Roll Over Shoulder
Tumbling

Purpose

Develop total-body agility and kinesthetic awareness

Procedure

- Start in a two-point stance with the left foot forward.
- Bend over and start to fall forward.
- As you are about to make contact with the ground, roll over the left shoulder.
- Roll and come back up to your feet.
- Perform forward rolls over both shoulders and with either foot forward.

Complex Variations

- Add a sprint in any direction before or after the tumbling drill.
- React to any stimuli after tumbling (for example, a visual cue to run to a cone).
- Add a sport-specific skill after tumbling.

Backward Roll Over Shoulder
Tumbling

Purpose
Develop total-body agility and kinesthetic awareness

Procedure
- Start in a two-point stance.
- Bend the legs and start to sit on the ground behind you.
- As you are about to make contact with the ground, roll back over the left shoulder.
- Continue to roll and come back up to your feet.
- Perform backward rolls over both shoulders.

Complex Variations
- Add a sprint in any direction before or after the tumbling drill.
- React to any stimuli after tumbling (for example, a visual cue to run to a cone).
- Add a sport-specific skill after tumbling.

Backward Roll
to Hand Push-Off
Tumbling

Purpose
Develop total-body agility and kinesthetic awareness

Procedure
- Start in a two-point stance.
- Bend the legs and start to sit on the ground behind you.
- As you are about to make contact with the ground, roll back.
- Continue to roll, and as your feet come over your head, push off using your hands and land on your feet.

Complex Variations
- Add a sprint in any direction before or after the tumbling drill.
- React to any stimuli after tumbling (for example, a visual cue to run to a cone).
- Add a sport-specific skill after tumbling.

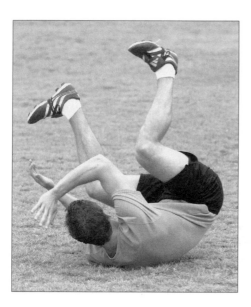

99

Forward Roll–Backward Roll Combination
Tumbling

Purpose

Develop total-body agility and kinesthetic awareness

Procedure

- Start in a two-point stance.
- Perform a forward roll to your feet.
- Immediately go into a backward roll with a hands push-off.
- You may start and end this drill on your knees to reduce amplitude and difficulty.

Complex Variations

- Add a sprint in any direction before or after the tumbling drill.
- React to any stimuli after tumbling (for example, a visual cue to run to a cone).
- Add a sport-specific skill after tumbling.

Cartwheel
Tumbling

Purpose
Develop total-body agility and kinesthetic awareness

Procedure
- Start in a two-point stance.
- Flex laterally to the left and put your left hand on the ground.
- Continue to turn, putting your right hand on the other side of the left hand.
- As your feet go over you, the right foot lands and then the left foot lands on the other side.
- Perform the drill to both sides.

Complex Variations
- Add a sprint in any direction before or after the tumbling drill.
- React to any stimuli after tumbling (for example, a visual cue to run to a cone).
- Add a sport-specific skill after tumbling.

Round-Off

Tumbling

Purpose

Develop total-body agility and kinesthetic awareness

Procedure

- Start in a two-point stance.
- Flex laterally to the left and put your left hand on the ground.
- Continue to turn, putting your right hand on the other side of the left hand while bringing your feet over you.
- As your feet go over you, rotate your body and land with both feet facing the starting position.
- Perform the drill to both sides.

Complex Variations

- Add a sprint in any direction before or after the tumbling drill.
- React to any stimuli after tumbling (for example, a visual cue to run to a cone).
- Add a sport-specific skill after tumbling.

Tumbling Drill Variations
Tumbling

Purpose

Develop total-body agility and kinesthetic awareness

Procedure

- Running Start and Tumbling Over Barrier: Perform all of the previous tumbling drills with a running start and tumble over a barrier; this will increase the amplitude and difficulty of the drill.

- Tumbling Sequencing: String two or more of the tumbling drills together; this will increase the kinesthetic demands of the drill by requiring additional coordination and kinesthetics.

Complex Variations

- Add a sprint in any direction before or after the tumbling drill.

- React to any stimuli after tumbling (for example, a visual cue to run to a cone).

- Add a sport-specific skill after tumbling.

Drop and Get Up
Crazy Z-Ball Drill

Purpose
Improve ability to change direction and reaction time

Procedure
- Throw a Crazy Z-ball up in the air.
- Get onto the ground, perform a push-up, and get to the ball before it bounces twice.
- This drill can also be done by trying to get the ball before its first bounce.
- This can also start with a partner releasing the ball and you on the ground.

Hexagon Drill

Hex-and-Dot Drill

Purpose

Improve agility

Procedure

- Each side of a hexagon is about 2 feet (61 centimeters) long, although this can vary.
- Begin in the middle of the hexagon facing a determined direction.
- Always facing that direction, jump with both feet outside each side of the hexagon.
- This should be done in both a clockwise and counterclockwise direction while being timed.

Complex Variations

- Use single-leg hops.
- Vary the size of the hexagon.

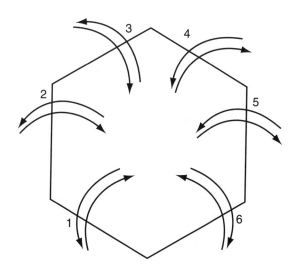

105

Toss, Get Up, and Catch
Medicine-Ball Drill

Purpose
Improve level-change capability; enhance transition from power to agility

Procedure

- Lie down on your back.
- Hold a medicine ball in your hands.
- Perform a chest pass into the air.
- Scramble up and catch the ball before it hits the ground.

Single-Leg Balance
With Opposite-Leg Reach

Purpose

Increase single-leg balance

Procedure

In the following set of drills, the opposite leg is used as a driver. Repeat all drills with a right-side stance and a left-leg reach.

- Left-leg balance with a right-leg anterior reach: Standing on your left leg, reach forward with your right leg as far as possible without loss of balance. Return to the starting position without touching the right foot to the ground. Attempt to complete all reps without the right foot contacting the ground.

- Left-leg balance with a right-leg posterior reach: Standing on your left leg, reach backward with your right leg as far as possible without loss of balance. Return to the starting position without touching the right foot to the ground. Attempt to complete all reps without the right foot contacting the ground.

- Left-leg balance with right-leg medial reach: Standing on your left leg, reach medially with your right leg as far as possible without loss of balance. Return to the starting position without touching the right foot to the ground. Attempt to complete all reps without the right foot contacting the ground.

Single-Leg Balance
With Opposite-Arm Reach

Purpose

Increase single-leg balance

Procedure

In the following set of drills, the arms are used as drivers. Reaches can be performed to foot, waist, or shoulder height. For all drills, attempt to complete all reps without the opposite foot contacting the ground. Remember to repeat all drills with a right-side stance.

- Left-leg balance, both arms anterior reach at waist height: Standing on your left leg, reach both arms at waist height as far forward as possible without losing balance. Return to the starting position.

- Left-leg balance, both arms anterior/medial reach at waist height: Standing on your left leg, reach both arms at waist height as far down an anterior/medial vector as possible without losing balance. Return to the starting position.

- Left-leg balance, both arms anterior/lateral reach at waist height: Standing on your left leg, reach both arms at waist height as far down an anterior/lateral vector as possible without losing balance. Return to the starting position.

- Left-leg balance, both arms posterior overhead reach: Standing on your left leg, reach both arms back over your head as far as possible without losing balance. Return to the starting position.

- Left-leg balance with opposite-arm multivector reach at foot height: Standing on your left leg, reach the opposite arm as far forward toward a given vector as possible without losing balance. Return to the starting position.

- Left-leg balance with same-side-arm multivector reach at foot height: Standing on your left leg, reach the same-side arm as far forward toward a given vector as possible without losing balance. Return to the starting position.

108

Single-Leg Balance
Dumbbell Presses

Purpose

Increase single-leg balance with resistance

Procedure

- This drill should be performed using a variety of tri-plane presses.
- Balancing on a single leg, perform overhead dumbbell presses through a variety of patterns.

Balance

Balance

133

Hop-and-Stick Balance Drills

These drills are dynamic in nature and closely resemble the balance required on the playing field. The possible number of variations to this drill is great, so only a few are covered here.

Purpose

Increase the ability to maintain balance in a dynamic situation

Procedure

These drills can be performed over a distance of 10 to 15 yards (9 to 14 meters). The stick-and-hold drill can be performed on whatever count the athlete and coach decide on—every one, every other, every third, and so on—or it can be performed on an audible call made by the coach or a training partner. Add head turning (that is, shaking your head no) to all movements to increase the level of difficultly.

- Forward hop and stick: Hop forward for 10 yards (9 meters); stick and hold on every other landing.
- Lateral hop and stick: Hop laterally for 10 yards (9 meters); stick and hold on every third landing.
- Medial hop and stick: Hop medially for 10 yards (9 meters); stick and hold landing on a verbal command.
- Forward side-to-side hop and stick: Hop forward using a side-to-side hop for 10 yards (9 meters); stick and hold on every third landing.

Lunge Patterns

Purpose

Increase lower extremity strength in three planes of motion; increase range of motion of the hips; and improve dynamic balance

Procedure

Standing in a tall upright posture, step forward into an anterior lunge, to the side for a lateral lunge, or rotationally for a transverse lunge. Return to the start position by pushing off strongly, being careful not to drag the foot when returning to the start.

Complex Variations

- Add dumbbells and reach for your foot.
- Throw your arms over your head while holding a medicine ball.
- Close your eyes.
- Shake your head no.

Balance

Chapter 5

© Nigel Farrow

Quickness and Reaction-Time Training

Diane Vives and Jim Roberts

Successful performance by an athlete depends heavily on his or her ability to react quickly. In sports performance, this usually requires the athlete to quickly decelerate and just as quickly accelerate. Whether it involves reacting to a starter's pistol at the beginning of a running race, out-jumping an opponent for a rebound on the basketball court, or being able to juke an opponent on the football field, the athlete with greater quickness and better reaction time (RT) usually maintains a competitive advantage.

Speed, rapidity, and instancy are all words that are used in defining quickness. All these terms refer to the rate of movement of an object, or the measurement of the distance it has traveled in a certain amount of time. When an athlete performs a task or a movement in a relatively brief period of time, he or she is described as being *quick.*

In and of itself, quickness seems simple enough to understand. An athlete is either quick or not, right? Wrong! Although it is true that genetic potential plays an important role in an athlete's physical abilities, many biomotor skills that contribute to quickness can be developed through training.

When discussing quickness, such factors as speed, acceleration, and agility are not always clearly distinguished: "Did you see how *quickly* he accelerated?" "It's amazing how *quickly* she made those cuts!" "Notice the *quick* leg turnover in that sprinter." All these factors are, of course, to some degree interconnected with quickness. But are they merely components of quickness, or is quickness instead something that can be trained and improved separately to promote successful athletic performance?

RT, which is predicated on one's ability to react quickly to a stimulus, also plays a major role in many sports. How quickly a hockey player can react to the drop of a puck will determine what percentage of face-offs he or she can win. Can we improve our RT?

The answer in both cases is yes. In this chapter, we will discuss how sport-specific quickness and RT can be improved. We will present exercises and drills, both simple to complex, that can be employed specifically for this purpose and that apply to a wide variety of sports-related movements.

Developing Quickness Skills

Athletes perform certain biomotor skills with an end result or purpose in mind. These "experienced" skills are recorded as memories of the varying patterns of movements, primarily in the sensory, sensory-association, and motor-control areas of the brain. These memories are referred to as sensory *engrams* of the movement patterns. Success with learning these skills is probably achieved through successive performance of the same skill activity until an engram for the movement is created (Guyton 1991).

New movements will always take a bit longer to improve on while their patterns are burned into an engram. If performed slowly, even highly complex motor skills can be accomplished the first time through. The movement must be slow enough at first for sensory feedback to occur. This allows proper adjustments to be made that serve as guides for improvement. However, when faced with having to learn quick athletic movements, one must always perform the biomotor patterns associated with the movements quickly. In any case, movements that have been repeatedly performed before can be recalled from memory. Without needing to focus on learning the patterns associated with these movements, the athlete can place particular emphasis on performing them at speed.

Training for Quickness

In considering training progression, coaches can employ simple drills to help athletes improve their ability to be aware of the intricacies involved in movement generally, as well as to help them enhance their level of skill with stopping and maintaining correct body position, optimal body angles, plant-foot position, and control of their center of mass. Coaches can also emphasize improving their athletes' ability to stop with good body position and control, decrease the time it takes for them to begin accelerating (that is, the amortization phase), and then immediately accelerate. By making an athlete *conscious* of successful movement strategies, over time and through numerous successful attempts he or she will begin to feel that these movement patterns become more *unconscious,* or "second nature" (Remedios and Liston 2003). The focus here should be on progression, precision, and repetition.

After an athlete masters the more basic patterns of movement, the coach can focus on the true nature of sport-specific "quickness," which involves the athlete performing skills with multiple or chaotic stimuli intended to increase reactive demands. More advanced drills with more complex decision-making requirements (such as open drills that include an increase in chaotic patterns) mimic the more unpredictable environment found in the sporting arena. By performing these drills, the athlete can continue to progressively respond to increased reactive and physical demands.

When training for quickness, keep in mind that the movements athletes perform when doing drills should always progress from

- slow to fast,
- simple to complex,
- active to reactive,
- predictable to unpredictable (in terms of reactive demands), and
- low-level to high-level plyometrics.

Reaction-Time Training

RT can be considered the precursor of quickness. In other words, the athlete must first see and recognize the need to react to an opposing player, for example, then he or she must move at a high speed to accomplish the task at hand. Considering most decisions in the athletic arena occur in 200 milliseconds or less, enhancing mental processing time should be viewed as equal in importance to the training program that is implemented (Prentice and Voight 1999; Schmidt and Lee 1998). In fact, it is arguable that mental processing speed is the sole defining feature of athletic greatness! Think about it. At the upper level of athletics, everyone is gifted physically. Take professional basketball players, for example. Relative to each position, most of these athletes possess similar physical gifts: similar speed, strength, and jumping ability. Yet, there is a distinct separation between the 98 percent who are merely great and the 2 percent who are truly exceptional. How is this possible? Why do athletes who possess similar physical gifts vary so widely in performance? Current research suggests that focusing on mental processing speed or RT gets us closer to answering this question; it suggests that mind speed is the new frontier in athletic development.

It is important to differentiate some key variables that comprise what is often mistakenly referred to as RT. RT is defined as the length of time it takes to initiate a movement. It includes the sensation and perception of a stimulus, and the selection of an appropriate response to the stimulus. But it does *not* include the movement itself. Movement time describes the time in which an action is taken, whether it is successful or not, relative to the stimulus or signal. Consequently, when describing athletic movement, it is more accurate to describe an athlete's reaction to a signal in terms of *total response time.* Total response time takes into account the mental processing time as well as the duration to perform the specific movement. Let's take a closer look at the components that comprise total response time.

Total response time can be broken down into two components: mental processing speed and movement time. The section that follows describes these two components and the various stages associated with each. Practical examples are provided to help you understand each component better.

Mental Processing Speed

Mental processing speed is composed of three stages: sensation, perception, and response selection.

• Sensation. During the sensation stage, an environmental stimulus acts on the athlete's body. As a result, an electric impulse is sent to the brain for extensive processing. The interval of time that elapses while the athlete detects the sensory input (light, sound, touch, and so on) from an object or the environment is referred to as *sensation time* (Green 1999). Let's consider the example of a volleyball serve-receive to put sensation time into a practical context. During a serve-receive, all six athletes on the receiving team must prepare to receive the ball. Each athlete must detect not only if the ball is coming toward him or her but also at what speed and with what characteristics. In this case, the visual amalgamation of colors and borders of the ball and the environment begins to reveal such characteristics of the ball as its direction, velocity, and disposition (Schmidt and Wrisberg 2000). Discerning these initial stimuli in the sensation stage begins to give meaning to the situation presented to the athlete and ushers in the second stage of mental processing speed, perception.

• Perception. During the perception stage, the results of the sensation stage are further processed, resulting in usable patterns of object movement that bring fuller meaning to the athlete's situation. The length of time needed to acknowledge and correlate the array of sensations discovered in stage one is defined as *perception time* (Green 1999). Continuing with our volleyball serve-receive example, all six athletes combine the visual amalgamation that has begun to be given meaning with the audible cues given by the defensive specialist to detect the serve as a deep, right-corner floater (note that audible cues register faster than visual stimuli) (Schmidt and Wrisberg 2000). At this point, each athlete must decide if a response is necessary. The information gathered in the perception stage is then passed on to the third stage of mental processing speed, response selection.

• Response selection. During the response-selection stage, the athlete decides whether or not a response is necessary to address the stimulus. In the volleyball example, all six players have detected that the serve is a deep, right-corner floater. As a result, five players will decide no response is necessary while one player must respond in a manner that results in proper body position for a successful pass. The total time required to organize a response, or the decision not to respond, to the environmental stimuli is called *response selection time* (Green 1999). Please note, for the sake of simplicity, that the serve-receive example describes the decision process involved in assessing whether or not to receive the serve. It does not consider off-ball movements that are required of the other five players on the court.

Movement Time

The second component of total response time, as noted previously, is movement time. Movement time is the time required to initiate and complete a specific movement or task. It involves the mechanisms in the brain stem and spinal cord that have to do with neuromuscular organization, as well as the actual orchestration of the muscles required for adequate force production, force reduction, force stabilization, and timing (Clark 2001; Schmidt and Wrisberg 2000). It is important to understand that movement time describes the time to initiate and complete a specific movement. It does not describe whether or not that movement achieves the desired objective, such as making contact with the ball during a serve-receive.

Factors Affecting Total Response Time

Although psychologists use the stages-of-processing model described in the previous section to simplify the explanation of motor activity, in reality this process is a continuous cycle of stimulus action/reaction and a resulting evaluation performed by the central nervous system. This cycle occurs to improve neuromuscular efficiency. Because of the interrelated properties that compose total response time, any improvement in the operation of one or more of the stages will enhance total response time. Likewise, any weakening of the operation of one or more of the stages will be detrimental to it. Described in the following section are the three most influential factors directly affecting RT, thus total response time. It becomes easy to see that achieving good mental processing speed is not only preferable in sports but absolutely essential—and that it can be improved through appropriate training.

Stimulus Choices

One of the most influential factors affecting RT is the number of possible stimulus choices that are presented at a given time. In this section, we will discuss the three different types of response selections—simple, choice, and recognition—and provide practical examples of each.

- A *simple reaction* is the fastest of the three types of reactions. In this situation, there is only one impending signal with one corresponding response. An example of this sort of reaction is the response athletes make when hearing the starter's gun at a swim meet. Because of the simplicity of the reaction, athletes often try to anticipate when the signal will occur to decrease their processing time, thus their RT. As a result, most competitions employ foreperiods and/or catch trials, in conjunction with predetermined "normal" RT standards (100 milliseconds is the Olympic standard), to determine whether or not an athlete anticipated or reacted to the signal.

- When an athlete is confronted with a *choice reaction,* there are two essential components that must be processed that are not required during a simple reaction: signal distinction and response selection (Green 1999). The former term refers to determining which signal occurred and the latter to selecting an appropriate response based on signal specificity. Choice reaction time is determined by the interval of time that elapses from the presentation of one of several possible unanticipated signals to the beginning of one of several possible responses (Schmidt and Lee 1998; Schmidt and Wrisberg 2000). As the number of possible signal-response pairs increases—that is, the number of choices an athlete is presented at any given time—the time required to respond to any one of them increases (Hick 1952). Thus, perception time is longer and, consequently, RT is slower.

- *Recognition reaction* comes into play in situations where there are various impending signals but only one correct response. In this situation, the athlete initiates a reaction when one signal occurs but declines to react when others are presented. Hence, RT is slower than choice reactions and substantially slower than simple reactions.

Anticipation

At this point, one might think that the athlete will be plagued by prolonged RTs. But in reality there is an abundance of information readily available to the vigilant athlete that can be used to plan and process future movements. Two essential means of combating potentially long RT are to anticipate *what* and *when* particular events are likely to occur. Psychologists use the terms spatial and temporal anticipation, respectively, to describe these two strategies.

- Spatial anticipation, also referred to as event anticipation, is defined as the capacity of an athlete to predict what is going to occur in a given situation (Schmidt and Lee 1998; Schmidt and Wrisberg 2000). This strategy allows the athlete to pre-plan his or her future movements with respect to a signal and therefore to eliminate stages two and three of mental processing speed. When successfully accomplished, spatial anticipation provides the athlete with a tremendous advantage, reducing RT by as much as 40 to 80 milliseconds (Schmidt and Wrisberg 2000). However, when executed erroneously, this strategy results in devastating consequences, often costing the athlete as much as 200 to 300 milliseconds of RT (Prentice and Voight 1999). An example of spatial anticipation is seen on the soccer field during a penalty kick. In this event, for instance, the goalie anticipates the kicker placing the ball in the upper-right side of the goal. As a result, the goalie jumps to the upper quadrant preparing for the block expecting he or she has guessed correctly. If the goalie's preplanned movement is correct, he or she arrives in time to block the ball. But if the athlete's preplanned movement is incorrect, the tax is much heavier than the 200 to 300 ms of RT typically associated with erroneous spatial anticipation. In this situation, the consequence is a point scored.

- Temporal anticipation is defined as the capacity of an athlete to predict when an event is going to occur during a given situation (Schmidt and Lee 1998; Schmidt and Wrisberg 2000). The tactical interaction that occurs in football between the quarterback and the defensive linemen during the snap is a good example of this strategy. During the snap, the quarterback uses a well-orchestrated presentation of visual and audible cues to attempt to draw his opponents offside while communicating to his offense when to move. If the quarterback did not randomize his or her snap count, the defense would have the advantage of knowing when to initiate their attack. As it is, the defense is forced to react to the movement of the ball, giving the offense the upper hand.

As one can see, the combination of both spatial and temporal anticipation allows the seasoned athlete to initiate his or her movements faster or at a time that is more relevant with respect to the demands of the environment (Schmidt and Lee 1998). For the sake of simplicity, both practical applications of these strategies described above were presented as isolated events. But in reality, the athlete's playing environment is a continual flow of audible, visual, and tactile signals from which he or she must readily detect and process those cues that can gain him or her the competitive edge over the opponent. It is this ability to efficiently interpret the continual flow of signals stemming from the environment that allows the best athletes to complete one action while processing the next, and quite possibly the one after that (Jeeves 1961; Leonard 1953; Prentice and Voight 1999; Schmidt and Lee 1998; Schmidt and Wrisberg 2000).

Skill-Specific Practice

The law of specificity states that the degree of performance adaptation that occurs during training is strongly related to the mechanical, neuromuscular, and metabolic similarity of the training program to competition itself (Clark 2001). In other words, the more similar the practice is to the actual activity for which the athlete is training in terms of movement mechanics, movement velocity, energy metabolism, and cardiorespiratory function, the greater the transfer of the training effect (Clark 2001). Therefore, if a baseball player needs to improve his or her ability to hit a baseball, the best activity to prescribe is typically batting practice.

With respect to total response time, the amount of skill-specific practice and the relativity of the practice to functional application are the two primary elements that govern choice response time. Simply stated, greater amounts of skill-specific practice produce shorter processing times and faster choice reaction times and are affected less by signal-response alternatives. The implementation of repetitive functional training will stimulate the conversion of conscious programming to unconscious programming (Prentice and Voight 1999). As a result, the response to a given stimulus is stored as a triggered response and is ultimately performed without continuous reference to conscious processes (Clark 2001; Prentice and Voight 1999). Triggered responses offer the trained athlete a tremendous advantage because they are extremely quick and are affected minimally as signal-response choices increase.

Drills for Quickness and Reaction Time

As described before, skills developed to enhance quickness and game-performance RT are most successful when they are task specific. The added experience of position-specific practice increases the athlete's ability to extract relevant information from his or her environment, resulting in quick and highly accurate response selections during different game situations. Practice of this sort also allows the trained athlete to cancel out false signals; eliminate distracting audible, visual, and mental "noise" from his or her environment; and reduce perception and response-selection time. All this can be accomplished while increasing the accuracy of movement selection for various environmental signals. It is important to understand that as the intensity of the environment increases—that is, as the athlete perceives greater stress and corresponding anxiety—the athlete's tendency is to resort back to preplanned motor programs regardless of appropriateness of the response. This is why task-specific practice coupled with "real time" mental processing demands is vital to improving quickness and RT at any level of athletics.

Having said this, and understanding that skills developed to enhance quickness and game-performance RT must be engrained on the microlevel, there are still a number of ways to incorporate the factors discussed in this chapter into the macrolevel to improve general RT and enhance overall athleticism through body quickness and increased speed. Keep in mind the law of specificity in your exercise prescription, and tailor the exercises you choose with your specific needs in mind.

Backpedal

Assorted Biomotor Skills

Purpose
Improve quickness and flexibility in the hip flexors

Procedure
- In an athletic stance, maintain your center of gravity over your base of support and run backward.
- Increase your stride length with good form.

Complex Variation
- On command, use an "open step" and sprint to a designated cone.

Quickness

Multidirectional Skipping
Assorted Biomotor Skills

Purpose
Improve quickness and coordination in locomotive mechanics

Procedure
- While skipping, respond to commands or cues to change your direction, using forward, backward, and side-skipping.
- Stay facing a target in front of you.

Complex Variations
- Increase the amplitude of your skip and lower the number of reps.
- Concentrate on the first skip after the command to change direction.
- Add a sprint or skill on command.

113

Medicine-Ball Bull in a Ring
Medicine-Ball Reaction

Purpose
Improve quickness and elastic strength

Procedure
- You and a partner face each other and chest pass a medicine ball while moving in a circle.

Medicine-Ball Lateral Shuffle/Pass

Medicine-Ball Reaction

Purpose

Improve quickness and elastic strength

Procedure

- You and a partner face each other. The distance you travel depends on the weight of the medicine ball: The lighter the ball, the farther you will travel.
- The drill begins with you both shuffling laterally while performing a chest pass back and forth along the predetermined route.
- Upon reaching the target distance, return in the opposite direction while continuing to pass the ball.

Complex Variation

- One of you leads and is free to change direction at will. The other athlete reacts and follows.

Quickness

115

Medicine-Ball Squat, Push Toss, Bounce, and Catch

Medicine-Ball Reaction

Purpose

Improve reactive, elastic strength, and total-body power

Procedure

- This drill is performed with a rubber medicine ball that can bounce.
- Begin by holding the ball chest high while squatting down and then throw the ball for height and distance.
- You must be quick enough to chase after the ball and catch it before it bounces twice.
- Obviously, a ball that is too light will travel too far, making it very difficult for you to retrieve it in time.

Medicine-Ball Forward Scoop Toss, Bounce, and Catch

Medicine-Ball Reaction

Purpose

Improve total-body power and reactive strength

Procedure

- The medicine ball is swung between your legs as you squat down and then thrown up and forward, releasing the ball at about shoulder height.
- Then sprint forward toward the ball to attempt to catch it before it bounces twice.

Quickness

Ball Drops With a Partner
Sports-Ball Reaction

Purpose
Improve visual stimulus response and first-step quickness

Procedure
- Using a ball, which can be specific to the target sport, have a partner stationed 5 to 10 yards (4.6 to 9 meters) away and drop the ball from shoulder height.
- Your partner must catch the ball after the first bounce but before a second bounce.

Complex Variations
- The height of the drop, or distance between partners, can be changed to accommodate skill level.
- You may choose to use a ball in each hand in order to increase the difficulty of responding.

Quickness

Goalie Drill

Sports-Ball Reaction

Purpose

Improve quickness in the upper body

Procedure

- A line and cones define a goal.
- You are the goalie, and a partner is the shooter.
- Your partner rolls the ball toward the goal.
- Try to stop the ball from crossing the line.
- You can use the hands, feet, or any combination to stop the ball from crossing the goal line.
- Switch roles and repeat.

Quickness

Partner Blind Tosses
Sports-Ball Reaction

Purpose
Improve upper- and lower-body quickness and reaction

Procedure
- While standing in a ready position, have a partner stand behind you and toss a tennis ball over one of your shoulders.
- Reacting as you see the ball, sprint and catch it before it bounces twice.

Complex Variation
- Perform this drill with a Crazy Z-ball.

Stability-Ball Cyclic Impact Lockouts

Stability-Ball Reaction

Purpose

Strengthen core and improve the body's ability to absorb impact

Procedure

- Assume a "hand-on-ball" push-up position.
- Keep the core (abs, lower back, and hips) tight.
- Release the ball, allowing yourself to fall on the ball.
- Make impact on the upper abdominals.
- As you bounce off the ball, secure it with the hands and lockout the arms.

Complex Variations

- Reach out and touch a target while bouncing.
- Clap your hands behind your body while bouncing.

121

Stability-Ball Hops
Stability-Ball Reaction

Purpose
Improve quickness in the upper-body pushing musculature

Procedure
- Placing your feet on the stability ball and hands on the floor (push-up position), begin to hop backward and forward and from side to side, maintaining your balance on the ball with your feet.
- Do not allow the abdominals and hips to sag. Maintain a firm body position.

Wheelbarrow Drill

Upper-Body Plyometrics

Purpose

Improve power in the upper body and core

Procedure

- A partner holds your feet while your hands perform a predetermined pattern or task.
- This should be done as quickly as possible while maintaining a straight body.
- It can be timed to judge improvements or your coach can encourage the use of visual cues, such as ladders, minihurdles, dot patterns, and so on.

Complex Variations

- Perform jumps instead of hand runs.
- Perform lateral shuffles or circular walks with the hands.

Note: All plyometric exercises can be initiated via a stimulus, such as a whistle blow, and can be preceded or followed by any skill (for example, catching a ball, sprinting, tumbling, and so on).

Plyo Push-Ups

Upper-Body Plyometrics

Purpose

Improve quickness in the upper-body pushing musculature

Procedure

- Beginning in the up position, perform an explosive push-up. The hands should leave the ground, achieving as much space between the hands and the ground as possible. Finish with the arms extended.
- When landing, keep your arms stiff, but not locked. Spend as little time on the ground as possible and explode back up.

Medicine-Ball Wall Chest Passes

Upper-Body Plyometrics

Purpose

Improve total-body transmission of power

Procedure

- Using a wall, perform chest passes to the wall and receive the ball with your arms extended before performing the next pass.
- This can be done for any number of repetitions, for time, or for distance.

Complex Variations

- Perform the drill with one arm.
- Perform it while moving laterally up and down the wall.

Quickness

125

Medicine-Ball Release Push-Ups With Partner

Upper-Body Plyometrics

Purpose

Improve quickness in the upper-body pushing musculature

Procedure

- Starting in a kneeling position, throw the medicine ball to a partner then fall into a push-up.
- Push up back into the start position while the partner returns the medicine ball. Repeat the exercise as quickly as possible.

Medicine-Ball Wall Side Toss
Upper-Body Plyometrics

Purpose
Enhance explosive rotational mechanics and changes in direction

Procedure
- Begin by facing the wall in an athletic position with a medicine ball held at your side.
- Throw the ball, striking the wall directly in front of you.

Complex Variations
- Use different stances, such as perpendicular to the wall.
- Use a parallel stance and toss the ball so that it rebounds to the other side of your body.

Quickness

127

Medicine-Ball Overhead Throw

Upper-Body Plyometrics

Purpose

Improve explosive power in throwing and overhead activities

Procedure

- Using a wall, load the ball over and behind the head with both hands, extending the entire body.
- Throw the ball at the wall with both hands and catch it with both hands.
- Keep a parallel stance and feet flat during the loading, or "cocking," phase.

Complex Variations

- Step forward while throwing (alternate legs).
- Throw from a kneeling position.

Medicine-Ball Wall Scoop Toss

Upper-Body Plyometrics

Purpose

Enhance total-body extension, quickness, and power

Procedure

- Face a wall in an upright athletic stance with a medicine ball.
- Quickly squat and extend your entire body.
- Toss the ball against the wall as fast as possible while maintaining a tight-backed, low-squat stance.
- Perform this drill for time or for a predetermined number of repetitions.

Complex Variations

- Perform a reverse scoop toss backward.
- Perform a long jump and then a scoop toss.

Quickness

Upper-Body Shuffles
Upper-Body Plyometrics

Purpose
Improve quickness in the upper-body pushing musculature

Procedure
- Beginning in the up position with your hands placed underneath each shoulder.
- Shuffle one hand up and one down as you drop into a push-up.
- Explosively push yourself up while exchanging hand positions in the air.

Complex Variation
- Start in the up position with your hands shoulder-width apart.
- Shuffle the hands out wider than the shoulders as you drop into a push-up.
- Explosively push up and shuffle the hands back underneath the shoulders while in the air.

Medicine-Ball One-Arm Push-Off

Upper-Body Plyometrics

Purpose

Improve power and quickness in the upper-body pushing musculature

Procedure

- Begin in a push-up position; your body should be straight with one hand on the medicine ball.
- Drop down into a push-up and explosively push off with the hand that is on the ground.
- The hand on the ball stays on it throughout the exercise. The hand pushing off the ground leaves the ground until it is at the same height or just above the height of the medicine ball.
- Be sure to lower the hand back to the ground in a controlled manner and then repeat the explosive push-off again once that hand makes contact with the ground.
- Your goal is to spend the least amount of time possible in contact with the ground by delivering an explosive push with the hand that is on the ground.

131

Medicine-Ball Upper-Body Shuffles

Upper-Body Plyometrics

Purpose

Improve power and quickness in the upper-body pushing musculature

Procedure

- Begin in a push-up position; your body should be straight with one hand on the medicine ball and your shoulders parallel to the floor.

- Drop down into a push-up and explosively push off laterally with the hands so that your body passes over the ball and the opposite hand lands on the ball.

- Your feet should remain about hip-width apart and your core should remain tight throughout the movement.

Upper-Body Box Shuffles
Upper-Body Plyometrics

Purpose

Improve power and quickness in the upper-body pushing musculature

Procedure

- Start in the push-up position with your hands on a box or step.
- Drop to the floor with your hands straddling the box.
- Explosively push off the floor to return hands to the top of the box.
- Try to get off the ground as quickly as possible.

Explosive Reclined Pulls
Upper-Body Plyometrics

Purpose

Improve power and quickness in the upper-body pulling musculature

Procedure

- Begin with a rope—at least 2 inches (5 centimeters) in diameter with a nonslippery surface—draped over a secured bar or through a secured hook.
- Hold onto the rope with the arm extended, your body reclined to 45 degrees and straight with a tight core.
- Explosively pull on the rope to quickly elevate your body and then regrip the rope.
- Repeat.

Quickness

Rope-Skipping
Lower-Body Plyometrics

Purpose
Improve quickness and elastic strength in the lower body

Procedure
- Skip rope while jumping to designated spots on the ground.
- This drill may be performed with both legs or a single leg.

Complex Variations
- Variable Patterns: Skip rope while changing patterns in response to commands. This variation may be performed with both legs or a single leg.
- Weighted Rope-Skipping: Perform the drill with a weighted rope.
- Side-Skipping: Perform the drill to the left or right. The arm and knee sequence should remain the same throughout. This drill can be the most challenging of all the skips.

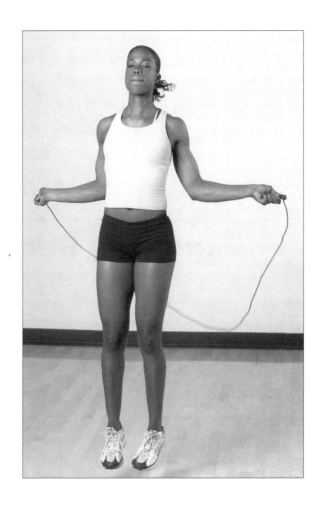

Quickness

In-Place Ankle Jumps
Lower-Body Plyometrics

Purpose
Improve elastic strength and quickness in the lower body

Procedure
- Perform in-place jumps just using the ankle.
- Spend a minimum amount of time on the ground.

Complex Variation
- Jump over a line on the ground, back and forth or sideways.

Quickness

Scissor Jumps

Lower-Body Plyometrics

Purpose

Improve quickness in hips; enhance balance

Procedure

- Begin by kicking one leg forward and up into the air as if punting a football.
- While in the air, leave the ground with the opposing leg and repeat with the opposite leg while the initial leg is returning to the ground.
- Repeat as quickly as possible for a predetermined number of reps or for time.
- Make sure you do the equivalent amount of work initiating the drill with the opposite leg.

Quickness

Lateral Skaters

Lower-Body Plyometrics

Purpose

Improve cutting ability and first-step lateral quickness

Procedure

- Begin with both feet together and push off laterally with one leg.
- Upon landing, immediately push off in the opposite direction and continue the drill for either reps or time.
- To develop quickness, perform as many reps as possible for time (10 seconds or less).

Complex Variation

- Jump diagonally so as to move laterally and forward.

Quickness

In-Place Tuck Jumps
Lower-Body Plyometrics

Purpose
Improve power in the lower body

Procedure

- Standing in the power position, load the lower body by swinging both arms back while flexing the hips and knees.
- Begin the extension of the hips and knees and finally the ankles as the arms swing forward but close to the body.
- Jump straight in the air, tucking both knees to the chest.
- Upon landing, repeat immediately with the same technique.
- For quickness, perform as rapidly as possible for time while counting reps, or for a fixed number of reps as rapidly as possible.
- This drill may be performed with a single leg as well.

Complex Variation

- Perform a pike jump, keeping your legs straight while tucking.

Quickness

Vertical Jump
Lower-Body Plyometrics

Purpose
Improve quickness and explosive power in the lower body

Procedure
- Stand with the feet shoulder-width apart (with the knees and hips flexed in a prestretched position and with the arms back and shoulders over the toes) and quickly dip into the power position.
- Perform a vertical jump by sequentially extending the ankles, knees, and hips, followed by reaching the arms straight up into the air.

Complex Variation
- Upon landing, immediately reload the legs and perform another vertical jump sequence, spending as little time as possible on the ground.

Quickness

140

Standing Long Jump
Lower-Body Plyometrics

Purpose
Improve lower-body power

Procedure
- Stand with both feet about shoulder-width apart or slightly narrower.
- Load the legs by flexing the knees and hips and cocking the arms backward.
- Propel your body up and out for distance by extending the legs and using the arms to help thrust the body forward for distance.

Barrier Jumps
Lower-Body Plyometrics

Purpose

Improve power and quickness in the lower body

Procedure

- Using something for a barrier (a hurdle, cones, boxes), propel your body over the barrier by jumping forward using an ankle-knee-hip extension.
- Maintaining a vertical body posture, tuck the knees to your chest while clearing the obstacle.
- Use a double-arm swing to maintain balance and assist in achieving vertical height.

Complex Variations

- Lateral Barrier Jumps: This variation is the same as Barrier Jumps except for the barrier now being conquered laterally. Begin by standing parallel to the barrier. Use the same loading action as described above, but now propel your body over the obstacle laterally. Upon landing, load the legs and arms once again and immediately jump laterally back over the barrier. Continue as quickly as possible for a set amount of jumps or for time.

- Single Leg Barrier Jumps: This variation is the same as Barrier Jumps but is performed with one leg at a time. This adds a great degree of difficulty to the jump and should be performed over shorter obstacles at first with gradual increases in height.

Power Skips
Lower-Body Plyometrics

Purpose
Improve lower-body power and quickness

Procedure
- Skip with an aggressive hip extension.
- The goal is to achieve increased distance and height with each skip.
- You should spend the least amount of time in contact with the ground as possible.

Lunge With Power-Up Jump
Lower-Body Plyometrics

Purpose
Improve lower-body power and quickness

Procedure
- Step into a lunge position and shift your weight toward your front leg.
- Drive off of the front leg into a forward motion and then land on two feet.
- Step out with the other leg and repeat.

144

Barrier Jump With Cut and Sprint

Lower-Body Plyometrics

Purpose

Improve lower-body power and quickness

Procedure

- Set up a barrier (such as a hurdle, cone, or bag) and two cones at 45-degree angles from the barrier and about 10 yards (9 meters) forward; your coach stands between the cones facing you.
- Jump over the barrier using the extension of your hip, knee, and ankle.
- While you are in the air, your coach gives either a visual or auditory signal to sprint to the left or right.
- As soon as your feet hit the ground, open your hip position and drive with your first step to sprint in the signaled direction.

Complex Variation

- After jumping the barrier, use a crossover step and sprint in the intended direction.

Push-Off Box Shuffle
Lower-Body Plyometrics

Purpose
Improve lower-body power and quickness

Procedure
- Use a box (or step) that rises no higher than halfway up your shin.
- Place one foot completely on the box and slightly lean forward so that your shoulders are over the edge of the box.
- Quickly push off the box with the foot that is on it and exchange feet in the air.
- The back foot should land with stiffness in the ankle to encourage an immediate rebound, or elastic response.
- The goal is to spend more time in the air and less time in contact with the box or the ground.

Quickness

146

Jump Rope With Multidirectional Jumps

Lower-Body Plyometrics

Purpose

Improve lower-body power and quickness

Procedure

- Jump rope while alternating between two foot positions.
- Start with a straddle position—that is, with the feet hip-width apart—then after you jump rope again, switch to a split-foot position with one foot up and one foot back.
- Continue to repeat this sequence as fast as you can.

Sequence Jumping Jacks

Lower-Body Plyometrics

Purpose

Improve lower-body power and quickness

Procedure

- Perform Jumping Jacks mixing a variety of arm and leg motions.
- Start with your feet hip-width apart and perform a jumping jack.
- Follow this by doing a jumping jack with the feet split forward and back, then return to the start position.
- Repeat.

Complex Variation

- Add a third Sequence Jump in which you land in a crossover foot position.

Quickness

Quick Feet (in All Directions)

Half Agility Ladder With Reaction Command

Purpose

Enhance stride frequency on the first step

Procedure

- Run through an agility ladder using a "one foot down between each rung" pattern.
- Concentrate on foot speed, not linear running speed.
- For variation, react to a command and run to a designated target.

Note: To avoid duplication, we have split the agility ladder drills between this chapter and chapter 4. Drills 148 through 152 emphasize short, "first-step" quickness. They employ half of a standard agility ladder to make the drill quicker and prevent neural fatigue from becoming a significant factor. Additionally, a reaction command will add the reaction/response component emphasized in this chapter.

Your coach can designate predetermined cones—for example, one cone on each side of the ladder, 5 to 10 yards (4.6 to 9 meters) from the ladder—for you to run to on receiving an audible or visual command. Every drill can be performed laterally or backward for increased difficulty.

Quickness

Bunny Jumps

Half Agility Ladder With Reaction Command

Purpose

Enhance elastic strength in the ankle complex

Procedure

- Perform fast multiple jumps into every square of the ladder.
- Use a quick ankling motion.
- Minimize ground contact.
- To add difficulty, a skill can be added to the drill.
- Look straight ahead, not at the ground.

150

Hop-Scotch Drill
Half Agility Ladder With Reaction Command

Purpose
Enhance elastic strength in the ankle complex

Procedure
- Start with one foot on each side of the ladder.
- Jump with both feet into the first space, then to the next space with feet spread apart so that each one lands on the outside of the ladder.
- Jump with both feet into the next square on the ladder.
- Keep repeating this.
- Look straight ahead, not at the ground.

Complex Variations
- Land on one foot when landing inside the ladder squares.
- To add difficulty, a skill can be added to the drill.

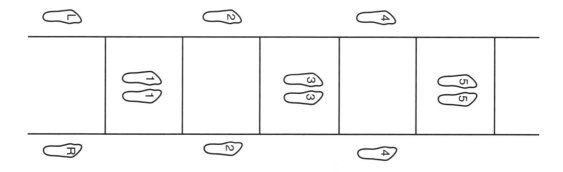

One-Leg Hop

Half Agility Ladder With Reaction Command

Purpose

Improve quickness in the lower body

Procedure

- Hop in every square, using only one leg.
- Emphasize minimizing ground contact.
- Look straight ahead, not at the ground.
- To add difficulty, a skill can be added to the drill.

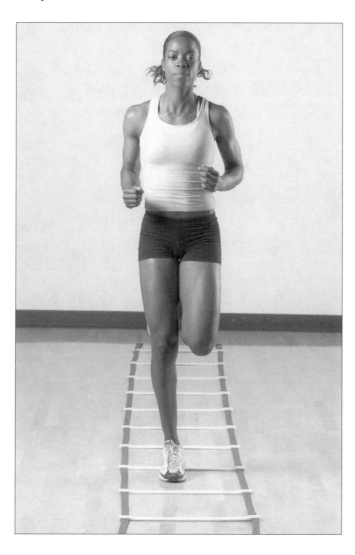

Half Ladder Skill to Sport-Specific Skill

Half Agility Ladder With Reaction Command

Purpose

Improve quickness in the lower body

Procedure

- You can perform any of the agility ladder drills while looking at your coach, who is positioned on the opposite side of the ladder.
- React to your coach throwing a sport-specific ball to either side of the ladder.
- React in mid-run to the side to which the ball is thrown and catch or hit the ball.

Quickness

Ruler Drop Test

Hand Quickness

Purpose

Improve upper-body quickness and reaction to a stimulus while providing feedback

Procedure

- Hold a ruler at shoulder height.
- Your partner holds his or her hand open with the arm extended.
- Your partner's thumb and index finger should be even with the "0" measurement at the end of the ruler.
- Release the ruler for your partner to catch as quickly as possible.
- The goal is to catch the ruler without letting it fall on the ground.

Quickness

154

Reactive Push-Ups With Clap
Upper-Body Reaction

Purpose
Improve upper-body power and reaction to stimulus

Procedure
- You and a partner are both in push-up position with your heads facing the same direction; you should be positioned 1 yard (.9 meter) apart.
- Perform a push-up with a clap.
- Your partner reacts to your movement, performing a push-up and attempting to clap at the same time you do.

Partner-Resisted Lateral Shuffle and Chase

Lower-Body Reaction

Purpose

Improve lower-body quickness and reaction; enhance ability to change direction

Procedure

- Start by facing a sideline in the athletic position, ready to side-shuffle.
- Your partner places a hand on the hip with which you will be leading the side-shuffle.
- On your coach's command, your partner resists your side-shuffle; your partner then lets go and sprints in same direction.
- Chase your partner and try to tag him or her as quickly as possible.

Quickness

156

Mirroring Partner Sprints
Lower-Body Reaction

Purpose
Improve ability to change direction

Procedure
- Set up lines or cones over a distance of approximately 20 yards (18 meters).
- Start on the start line with your partner 5 yards (4.6 meters) ahead and facing you.
- Sprint forward for 10 yards (9 meters) while your partner backpedals in front of you.
- Stop and backpedal as your partner stops and sprints forward 5 yards (4.6 meters); try to always maintain the same distance between you.
- Repeat the sequence until you reach the 20-yard (18-meter) line.

Containing-Opponent Drill

Lower-Body Reaction

Purpose

Improve ability to change direction and to react

Procedure

- Set up lines and cones over a distance of approximately 20 yards (18 meters) wide by 80 yards (73 meters) long.
- Stand on the end line to start.
- Three or four opponents face you in a line to act as a wall to contain you.
- The opponents backpedal as well as move side to side in order to prevent you from sprinting though their line.

Quickness

Mirroring Two-Box Drill
Lower-Body Reaction

Purpose
Improve ability to change direction and react

Procedure
- Mark two boxes with four cones each, with 5 yards (4.6 meters) between each cone.
- Begin by standing in one box while a partner stands in the other.
- Start in the middle of your box and sprint to any given cone, touch it, and return to the center of the box.
- Your partner must mirror you, reacting to your movements.

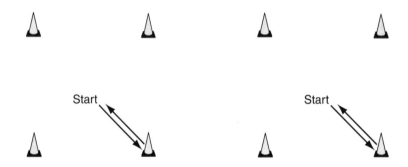

Quickness

Mirror Drills in Box
With Square Shuffle

Lower-Body Reaction

Purpose

Improve lower-body quickness in a lateral direction and ability to react

Procedure

- Mark two boxes with four cones each, with 5 yards (4.6 meters) between each cone (marked lines are preferable).
- You start as commander on the line of one box, and your partner starts on the same line of the other box.
- You can only shuffle on the outside of the box, staying on the lines.
- Your partner must react and mirror you by only shuffling on the same lines of his or her box.

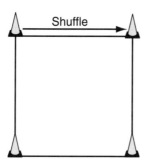

Quickness

160

Triangle Drills With Commands
Lower-Body Reaction

Purpose
Improve quickness of the foot plant and change of direction

Procedure
- Place three cones in a triangle with sides 5 yards apart.
- Start at the designated cone, sprinting as fast as possible.
- Stay close to the cones.
- Change the direction of the sprint after 2 to 4 turns based on the coach's verbal command.

Complex Variation
- Triangle Chase Drill—Stand on the line between two cones. Add a partner who is the chaser and starts at the third cone. Start the chase on the verbal command of the coach and finish when tagged by the chaser.

Three-Step Foot-Tap Drill With Sprint

Lower-Body Reaction With Hoops

Purpose

Improve quickness of first step and reaction

Procedure

- Start by standing outside of a hoop; quickly tap your foot twice outside the hoop then tap one foot laterally, touching inside the hoop.
- Tap inside the hoop with the foot closest to it.
- Your coach then gives a visual or auditory command; you must quickly take a step forward and sprint to a cone 5 yards (4.6 meters) in front of you, touch the cone, return to the beginning position, and continue with the original foot-tapping pattern.

Quickness

162

Three-Point Fire Drill With Reaction

Lower-Body Reaction With Hoops

Purpose

Improve lower-body quickness, reaction, and ability to change direction

Procedure

- Set up a box with hoops in each corner, spaced 10 yards (9 meters) from each other.
- Put two more hoops in the middle of the square about 1 yard (.9 meter) apart; you and a partner are in the middle of the box, one assigned to each hoop.
- Both of you start the drill using a fast tap, or "fire feet," while keeping one foot in your hoop.
- Your coach stands at the base of the box and gives visual signals (such as "hands up" or "hands down") to direct both of you to sprint to the back side of the hoop or the front side on your side of the square, to turn, and to sprint back to try to beat your partner to the start position.
- Always maintain a fast tap when returning to the start position.

Complex Variation

- Your coach can ask that you use hand touches in all hoops, requiring more total-body quickness.

Three-Step Foot-Tap Drill With Sprint Plus Ball Drop

Lower-Body Reaction With Hoops

Purpose

Improve quickness of the first step and upper-body reaction

Procedure

- Start by standing outside a hoop; quickly tap your foot twice outside the hoop and then tap your foot once laterally, touching inside the hoop.
- You should tap inside the hoop with the foot closest to the hoop.
- A partner stands 5 yards (4.6 meters) away and drops a tennis ball from shoulder height.
- You must quickly make a first step forward and sprint to catch the ball before it bounces twice.

Mirror Two-Box Drill With Switching Commander

Upper- and Lower-Body Reaction

Purpose

Improve total-body quickness and ability to change direction

Procedure

- Mark two boxes with four cones each, with 5 yards (4.6 meters) between each cone.
- You start as commander in one box with your partner in the other box.
- Start by making any move you choose (a squat, a side-shuffle, a jump, giant circles, sprinting and touching a cone, and so on).
- Your partner must react and follow your movements.
- At any time, your coach will give an audible signal and your partner will become the commander; now you must react and mirror.

Quickness

Directional Foot Movement
Quick Reaction

Purpose
Improve mental processing speed and first-step movement time

Procedure
- Move your foot in the direction of a stimulus (for example, a hand signal, foot signal, shoulder signal, or ball toss).
- Work only on your first-step reaction.

Complex Variations
- Add a second step, progressing to a full skill movement.
- Preplan a signal to which you respond, but have your coach give multiple signals.

Directional Hand Movement
Quick Reaction

Purpose
Improve mental processing speed and upper-body movement time

Procedure
- Move your hand in the direction of a stimulus (for example, a hand signal, shoulder signal, or ball pass).
- Work only on your hand reaction.

Complex Variations
- Add footwork to your hand-response work, progressing to a full skill movement.
- Preplan a signal to which you respond, but have your coach give multiple signals.

Reaction Time

Directional Mirror Drill
Quick Reaction

Purpose
Improve mental processing speed and quickness of movement time

Procedure
- This drill is performed with a partner.
- Perform all directional foot movements and variations.
- Initiate the leg or arm movements (or a combination of both); your partner reacts by mirroring the same movement.
- Switch roles and repeat.

Complex Variation
- Perform offensive or defensive mirroring with a training tool, such as a basketball.

Sprint and Backpedal on Command

Directional Change

Purpose

Improve reaction time and ability to change direction

Procedure

- Start in a two-point stance.
- On command, sprint.
- On the next command, backpedal.
- Repeat.

Complex Variations

- Start from different stances.
- Change biomotor skills throughout the drill or on each command.
- Add a plyometric exercise on each command.
- Vary the distances traveled between commands.

Reaction Time

Sprint and Cut on Command
Directional Change

Purpose
Improve mental processing speed, quickness of movement time, and ability to change direction

Procedure
- Start in a two-point stance.
- Sprint on command, cut sharply, and sprint in the instructed direction.

Complex Variations
- Start from different stances.
- Change biomotor skills throughout the drill or on each command.
- Add a plyometric exercise on each command.
- Vary the distances traveled between commands.
- Change the cut angle.

170

Backpedal and Cut on Command

Directional Change

Purpose

Improve mental processing speed, quickness of movement time, and ability to change direction

Procedure

- Start in a two-point stance.
- Backpedal on command, cut sharply, and sprint in the instructed direction.

Complex Variations

- Start from different stances.
- Change biomotor skills throughout the drill or on each command.
- Add a plyometric exercise on each command.
- Vary the distances traveled between commands.
- Change the cut angle.

Reaction Time

201

171

Star Drill
Directional Change

Purpose
Improve mental processing speed and multidirectional quickness

Procedure
- Stand in a hoop placed in the middle of an eight-hoop circle.
- Assume a ready position and wait for a signal.
- React to the signal and run to each hoop, putting one foot in the hoop.
- Run back until both feet are inside the middle hoop.

Complex Variations
- Start from different stances.
- Use a defensive lateral slide instead of a sprint.
- Add a skill movement on command (for example, sprawl on the whistle, intercept a passed ball, pass to a target, and so on).
- Vary the commands given both audibly and visually.

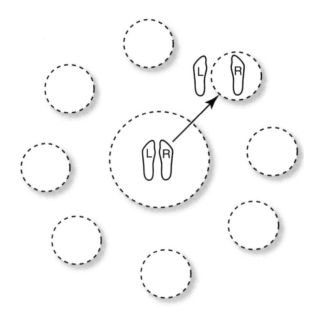

Four-Point Pop-Up
Four-Limb Quickness

Purpose

Improve mental processing speed, total-body agility, kinesthetic awareness, and quickness

Procedure

- Start on the ground on your hands and knees and wait for a signal.
- Explode as fast as possible as you stand up.

Complex Variations

- Follow standing up with a skill movement done on command.
- Follow standing up with a tennis-ball catch.

Sit-to-Stand Pop-Up
Four-Limb Quickness

Purpose
Improve mental processing speed, total-body agility, kinesthetic awareness, and quickness

Procedure
- Start from a sitting position on the ground and wait for a signal.
- Explode as fast as possible as you stand up.

Complex Variations
- Follow standing up with a skill movement done on command.
- Follow standing up with a tennis-ball catch.
- Vary the commands given both audibly and visually.

174

Lying-to-Stand Pop-Up
Four-Limb Quickness

Purpose
Improve mental processing speed, total-body agility, kinesthetic awareness, and quickness

Procedure
- Start from a lying position on the ground and wait for a signal.
- Explode as fast as possible as you stand up.

Complex Variations
- Follow standing up with a skill movement done on command.
- Follow standing up with a tennis-ball catch.
- Vary the commands given both audibly and visually.

175

Sprawl-to-Stand Pop-Up
Four-Limb Quickness

Purpose
Improve mental processing speed, total-body agility, kinesthetic awareness, and quickness

Procedure
- Start from a two-point stance and wait for a signal.
- Perform a sprawl and get up as quickly as possible.

Complex Variations
- Follow standing up with a skill movement done on command.
- Follow standing up with a tennis-ball catch.
- Vary the commands given both audibly and visually.

Reaction Time

Drop-and-Go Pop-Up

Four-Limb Quickness

Purpose

Improve mental processing speed, total-body agility, kinesthetic awareness, and quickness

Procedure

- Throw a ball in the air.
- Perform a sprawl and get up as quickly as possible.
- Catch the ball before it bounces twice.

Complex Variations

- Use a Crazy Z-ball to enhance your multidirectional reaction time.
- Have a partner throw the ball during your sprawl.

Reaction Time

Side-Shuffle
Lateral Speed

Purpose
Improve mental processing speed, lateral agility, and quickness

Procedure
- Begin in a ready position—your knees and hips slightly flexed, arms relaxed and to the sides, and shoulders over toes—and wait for a signal.
- Shuffle laterally in the direction of a command from your coach without crossing your feet.
- This should be done by accelerating and then decelerating in order to stop as soon as subsequent commands to change direction are given.

Complex Variations
- Use visual cues instead of audible cues.
- Have your coach move in a semicircle in front of you while you are shuffling to develop court sense.

Hot Hands
Hand Speed

Purpose

Improve mental processing speed, upper-body reaction time to visual stimuli, and quickness

Procedure

- Put your hands together (palm to palm) in front of you.
- A partner stands in front of you with the hands at his or her side.
- Your partner tries to quickly touch (that is, to lightly slap) your hands while you try to react and avoid being touched.

Complex Variation

- Both you and your partner assume a ready position.
- Follow the same procedure as stated above with two separate contact targets instead of one.

Ball Release
Hand Speed

Purpose

Improve mental processing speed, upper-body reaction time to visual stimuli, and quickness

Procedure

- Hold two tennis balls out in front of you at shoulder height.
- A partner stands in front of you in a ready position.
- Release one of the two tennis balls without advance notice; your partner reacts and attempts to catch it in midair.

Complex Variations

- Have your partner use the contralateral hand to catch the tennis ball.
- Release both tennis balls simultaneously.

Reaction Time

Card-Snatching

Hand Speed

Purpose

Improve upper-body quickness and reaction ability to visual stimuli

Procedure

- Hold a playing card at shoulder height.
- A partner stands in front of you in a ready postion.
- Your partner initiates the drill by attempting to snatch the card out of your hand.
- React by attempting to move the card so as to prevent your partner from snatching it.

181

The Bob
Upper-Body Reaction

Purpose
Improve mental processing speed, upper-body reaction time to visual stimuli, and total-body quickness

Procedure
- Stand in a ready position or in a position particular to your sport.
- A partner stands in front of you.
- Using a foam bat, focus mitt, or an oversized boxing glove, your partner initiates the drill by attempting to lightly contact your head area.
- The attack is made along the sagittal plane (that is, straight on).
- Respond by avoiding contact, moving to either side of the attack.

182

The Parry
Upper-Body Reaction

Purpose
Improve mental processing speed, upper-body reaction time to visual stimuli, and total-body quickness

Procedure
- Stand in a ready position or in a position particular to your sport.
- A partner stands in front of you.
- Using a foam bat, focus mitt, or an oversized boxing glove, your partner initiates the drill by attempting to lightly contact your head area.
- The attack is made along the sagittal plane (that is, straight on).
- Respond by using your hands and slapping off the attack just before contact.

The Weave
Upper-Body Reaction

Purpose
Improve mental processing speed, upper-body reaction time to visual stimuli, and total-body quickness

Procedure
- Stand in the ready position or in a position particular to your sport.
- A partner stands in front of you.
- Using a foam bat, focus mitt, or an oversized boxing glove, your partner initiates the drill by attempting to lightly contact your head area.
- The attack is made along the sagittal plane or transverse plane (that is, straight on or via a roundhouse).
- Respond by ducking and weaving under the attack.

Focus Mitt
Upper-Body Speed

Purpose
Improve mental processing speed, upper-body reaction time to visual stimuli, hand–eye coordination, and total-body quickness

Procedure
- Stand in the ready position or in a position particular to your sport.
- A partner stands in front of you.
- Using a focus mitt, your partner initiates the drill by presenting the mitt as a target to which you are to deliver a predetermined punch or slap.
- Your attack may mimic sport-specific movements, such as a tennis forehand or football lineman's hand technique.

Complex Variations
- Add an additional mitt for complex response decisions.
- Throw multiple punches or combinations to specific targets.

Reaction Time

185

Dodge Ball
Whole-Body Reaction

Purpose

Improve mental processing speed and total-body reaction time to visual stimuli

Procedure

- This game can be played against a wall with two to four players or in a circle with five or more players.
- Using soft balls, multiple players throw while other players evade ball contact.

186

Rapid Fire
Whole-Body Reaction

Purpose

Improve mental processing speed, total-body reaction time to visual/audible stimuli, and total-body quickness

Procedure

- Assume a ready position and wait for a start signal.
- On the signal (either a visual or audible cue), begin to tap your feet alternately as fast as possible until the next command.
- React to each command (for example, to do a lateral shuffle, forward/backward sprint, jump, sprawl, and so on) as quickly as possible.

Barrel Roll to Reaction
Whole-Body Reaction

Purpose
Improve mental processing speed, total-body reaction time to visual/audible stimuli, and total-body agility

Procedure
- Start in a two-point stance with the left foot forward.
- Bend over and start to fall forward.
- Roll over on the left shoulder just before making contact with the floor.
- Roll and return to a ready position and react to your coach's audible or visual cue.

Complex Variation
- Add a sport-specific skill after the roll (such as a volleyball dig, right or left sprawl, cover tip, lateral shuffle, and so on).

Backward Roll to Reaction
Whole-Body Reaction

Purpose
Improve mental processing speed, total-body reaction time to visual/audible stimuli, and total-body agility

Procedure
- Start in a ready position.
- Squat, bend over, and start to fall backward.
- Roll over on the left or right shoulder and return to the ready position.
- React to your coach's audible or visual cue.

Complex Variation
- Add a sport-specific skill after the roll (such as a volleyball dig, right or left sprawl cover tip, lateral shuffle, and so on).

Reaction Time

189

Skiers With Reaction
Whole-Body Reaction

Purpose

Improve mental processing speed, court sense, total-body reaction time to visual/audible stimuli, total-body agility, and general athleticism

Procedure

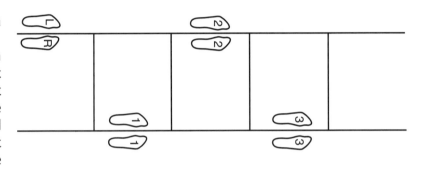

- Start in a two-point stance with the right foot inside the first square of the ladder and the left foot outside the first square.

- Jump forward and diagonally to the right and land the left foot inside the second square of the ladder and the right foot on the outside of the second square.

- Immediately upon landing, jump forward and diagonally to the left and land the right foot inside the third square of the ladder and the left foot on the outside of the third square.

- Repeat this sequence throughout the ladder while reacting to your coach's visual commands (for example, call out the number of fingers he or she holds up) continuously throughout the drill.

Complex Variations

- Add a sport-specific skill at the end of the ladder.
- Call out only odd or even numbers as your coach shows both.
- Your coach can work a semicircle around the end of the ladder to enhance your peripheral vision.
- Two or three coaches can compose the semicircle, flashing numbers as described above to further enhance your court vision and reaction times to stimuli on the periphery of your vision. Note that seeing objects with different sections of the eyes produce different reaction times. Stimuli picked up by the cones (or the nerves at the center of the eyes) register information faster than objects picked up by the rods (or nerves along the outside portion of the eyes). Practice reacting to stimuli on the periphery of your vision enhances reaction time to stimuli picked up in your central vision. Likewise, practice reacting to stimuli picked up in central vision enhances peripheral vision reaction time.
- Add a 2- to 3-step "run in" to increase linear speed and quickness requirements through the ladder.

Hop-Scotch With Reaction
Whole-Body Reaction

Purpose

Improve mental processing speed, court sense, total-body reaction time to visual/audible stimuli, total-body agility, general athleticism, and elastic strength in the ankle complex

Procedure

- Start with both feet inside the first square of the ladder.

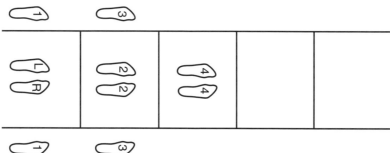

- Jump with both feet, landing each foot outside the ladder.

- Immediately upon landing, jump and land both feet inside the next square of the ladder.

- Repeat this sequence throughout the ladder while reacting to your coach's visual commands (for example, call out the number of fingers he or she holds up) continuously throughout the drill.

Complex Variations

- Add a sport-specific skill at the end of the ladder.
- Call out only odd or even numbers as your coach shows both.
- Your coach can work a semicircle around the end of the ladder to enhance your peripheral vision.
- Two or three coaches can compose the semicircle, flashing numbers as described above to further enhance your court vision and reaction times to stimuli on the periphery of your vision. Note that seeing objects with different sections of the eyes produce different reaction times. Stimuli picked up by the cones (or the nerves at the center of the eyes) register information faster than objects picked up by the rods (or nerves along the outside portion of the eyes). Practice reacting to stimuli on the periphery of your vision enhances reaction time to stimuli picked up in your central vision. Likewise, practice reacting to stimuli picked up in central vision enhances peripheral vision reaction time.
- Add a 2- to 3-step "run in" to increase linear speed and quickness requirements through the ladder.

Icky Shuffle With Reaction
Quick Feet

Purpose
Improve mental processing speed, court sense, total-body reaction time to visual/audible stimuli, total-body agility, and general athleticism

Procedure
- Start on the left side of an agility ladder.
- Step laterally with the right foot and place it in the first square of the ladder.
- Advance the left foot to be inside the same box.
- Step laterally with the right foot to the right side of the ladder and the left foot to its next square.
- Bring the right foot to the same square in which you have your left foot.
- Step laterally to the left of the ladder and advance the right foot to the next square. Repeat this pattern to the end of the ladder.
- React to your coach's visual commands (for example, call out the number of fingers he or she holds up) continuously throughout the drill.

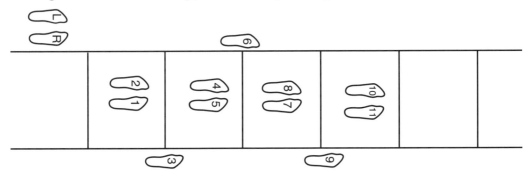

Complex Variations
- Add a sport-specific skill at the end of the ladder.
- Call out only odd or even numbers as your coach shows both.
- Your coach can work a semicircle around the end of the ladder to enhance your peripheral vision.
- Two or three coaches can compose the semicircle, flashing numbers as described above to further enhance your court vision and reaction times to stimuli on the periphery of your vision. Note that seeing objects with different sections of the eyes produce different reaction times. Stimuli picked up by the cones (or the nerves at the center of the eyes) register information faster than objects picked up by the rods (or nerves along the outside portion of the eyes). Practice reacting to stimuli on the periphery of your vision enhances reaction time to stimuli picked up in your central vision. Likewise, practice reacting to stimuli picked up in central vision enhances peripheral vision reaction time.
- Add a 2- to 3-step "run in" to increase linear speed and quickness requirements through the ladder.

Reaction Time

Backward Icky Shuffle With Reaction

Quick Feet

Purpose

Improve mental processing speed, court sense, total-body reaction time to visual/audible stimuli, total-body agility, and general athleticism

Procedure

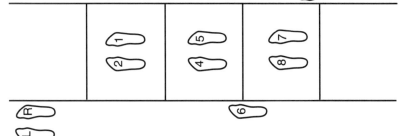

- Start on the right side of an agility ladder, facing backward.
- Step laterally with the right foot and place it in the first square of the ladder.
- Step with the left foot to be inside the same box.
- Step laterally and drop-step with the right foot to the right side of the ladder and step back with the left foot to its next square.
- Bring the right foot to the square in which you have your left foot.
- Step laterally and drop-step to the left side of the ladder and step back with the right foot to its next square. Repeat this pattern to the end of the ladder.
- React to your coach's visual commands (for example, call out the number of fingers he or she holds up) continuously throughout the drill.

Complex Variations

- Add a sport-specific skill at the end of the ladder.
- Call out only odd or even numbers as your coach shows both.
- Your coach can work a semicircle around the end of the ladder to enhance your peripheral vision.
- Two or three coaches can compose the semicircle, flashing numbers as described above to further enhance your court vision and reaction times to stimuli on the periphery of your vision. Note that seeing objects with different sections of the eyes produce different reaction times. Stimuli picked up by the cones (or the nerves at the center of the eyes) register information faster than objects picked up by the rods (or nerves along the outside portion of the eyes). Practice reacting to stimuli on the periphery of your vision enhances reaction time to stimuli picked up in your central vision. Likewise, practice reacting to stimuli picked up in central vision enhances peripheral vision reaction time.

Reaction Time

In-and-Out Shuffle With Reaction
Quick Feet

Purpose

Improve mental processing speed, court sense, total-body reaction time to visual/audible stimuli, total-body agility, and general athleticism

Procedure

- Start in a two-point stance facing one side of the ladder.

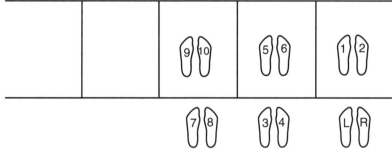

- Step with the left foot straight ahead into the first square.

- Follow with the right foot into the first square.
- Step back and diagonally with the left foot until it is in front of the second square.
- Follow with the right foot until it is in front of the second square.
- Repeat this sequence throughout the ladder, making sure each foot hits each box.
- React to your coach's visual commands (for example, call out the number of fingers he or she holds up) continuously throughout the drill.

Complex Variations

- Add a sport-specific skill at the end of the ladder.
- Call out only odd or even numbers as your coach shows both.
- Your coach can work a semicircle around the end of the ladder to enhance your peripheral vision.
- Two or three coaches can compose the semicircle, flashing numbers as described above to further enhance your court vision and reaction times to stimuli on the periphery of your vision. Note that seeing objects with different sections of the eyes produce different reaction times. Stimuli picked up by the cones (or the nerves at the center of the eyes) register information faster than objects picked up by the rods (or nerves along the outside portion of the eyes). Practice reacting to stimuli on the periphery of your vision enhances reaction time to stimuli picked up in your central vision. Likewise, practice reacting to stimuli picked up in central vision enhances peripheral vision reaction time.

Snake With Reaction
Quick Feet

Purpose

Improve mental processing speed, court sense, total-body reaction time to visual/audible stimuli, total-body agility, general athleticism, and elastic strength in the ankle complex

Procedure

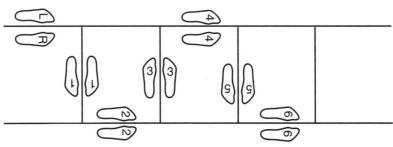

- Start in a two-point stance, straddling one side of the ladder.
- Keeping both feet together, perform a series of quarter-turn jumps.
- The direction the feet should point for each jump is as follows: straight ahead, right, straight ahead, left, straight ahead, and so on.
- Keep the shoulders relatively square while rotating the hips.
- Repeat this sequence throughout the ladder while reacting to your coach's visual commands (for example, call out the number of fingers he or she holds up) continuously throughout the drill.

Complex Variations

- Add a sport-specific skill at the end of the ladder.
- Call out only odd or even numbers as your coach shows both.
- Your coach can work a semicircle around the end of the ladder to enhance your peripheral vision.
- Two or three coaches can compose the semicircle, flashing numbers as described above to further enhance your court vision and reaction times to stimuli on the periphery of your vision. Note that seeing objects with different sections of the eyes produce different reaction times. Stimuli picked up by the cones (or the nerves at the center of the eyes) register information faster than objects picked up by the rods (or nerves along the outside portion of the eyes). Practice reacting to stimuli on the periphery of your vision enhances reaction time to stimuli picked up in your central vision. Likewise, practice reacting to stimuli picked up in central vision enhances peripheral vision reaction time.
- Add a 2- to 3-step "run in" to increase linear speed and quickness requirements through the ladder.

Chubby Checkers With Reaction
Quick Feet

Purpose

Improve mental processing speed, court sense, total-body reaction time to visual/audible stimuli, first-step quickness, and general athleticism

Procedure

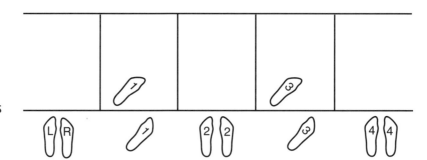

- Start in a two-point stance, facing the ladder on its far left side.

- Jump laterally to the right with both feet, landing the left foot inside the first square of the ladder and the right foot outside the first square.

- Immediately upon landing, jump laterally to the right with both feet landing outside the ladder.

- The hips should rotate so that the feet are diagonal to the ladder when the left foot is in the square and perpendicular to it when both feet are outside the ladder.

- Repeat this sequence while advancing the length of the ladder and reacting to your coach's visual commands (for example, call out the number of fingers he or she holds up) continuously throughout the drill.

Complex Variations

- Add a sport-specific skill at the end of the ladder.

- Call out only odd or even numbers as your coach shows both.

- Your coach can work a semicircle around the end of the ladder to enhance your peripheral vision.

- Two or three coaches can compose the semicircle, flashing numbers as described above to further enhance your court vision and reaction times to stimuli on the periphery of your vision. Note that seeing objects with different sections of the eyes produce different reaction times. Stimuli picked up by the cones (or the nerves at the center of the eyes) register information faster than objects picked up by the rods (or nerves along the outside portion of the eyes). Practice reacting to stimuli on the periphery of your vision enhances reaction time to stimuli picked up in your central vision. Likewise, practice reacting to stimuli picked up in central vision enhances peripheral vision reaction time.

Chapter 6

Designing Sport-Specific Training Programs

Vance Ferrigno, Lee E. Brown, and Daniel Murray

This final chapter is designed to give you examples of how to use the drills in this book. The sport-specific programs we have provided emphasize proper progression from basic to more complex speed, agility, and quickness drills. These programs are not intended to provide a "cookie-cutter" approach to program design. Every athlete has distinctive goals and needs, even those who play the same sport and position.

Speed, agility, balance, quickness, and reaction-time drills cover the complete spectrum of biomotor skill, from basic and low intensity to complex and high intensity. Some of the basic skills, like skipping, balance drills, and medicine-ball work, can be used while warming up for any training session. Other higher-intensity exercises, like high-intensity jumping drills, can put enormous stress on both physiological structures and the central nervous system (CNS). These drills should be used wisely, and ample recovery between drills and training sessions that employ them should be provided.

The information derived from the needs analysis section in chapter 2 is the key to properly designing a safe and effective speed, agility, and quickness program. Only after an athlete's limiters are determined can a program be designed specifically for them. Each workout must have a defined goal and each drill should be chosen to meet that goal. Training just to train and randomly choosing drills will not provide the results you are looking for. It is also important to remember the concept of specificity: speed, agility, and quickness training should attempt to closely mimic the movements performed by the athlete during competition. This will produce the greatest amount of improvement in performance.

Once you have decided on the major goals for the year, several mesocycles can be programmed to more specifically address the objectives of the training program. The programs we have provided use mesocycles geared toward improving speed, agility, and quickness in various sports. Each mesocycle consists of six microcycles, each one week in duration. Adjustments can and should always be made to each microcycle to ensure that the training program stays on track and that consistent and safe progress is made.

It is important to note that speed, agility, and quickness training is just one segment of the total training plan, which also includes training for functional strength, flexibility, and proper restoration. Any of these components may be emphasized, depending on where you are in your athletic development or training cycle. For our purposes in this chapter, we assume that the major emphasis for the current mesocycle is speed, agility, and quickness. We also assume that basic locomotive mechanics have been mastered and that general conditioning has been completed.

Determining Program Elements

There are many variables that factor in when designing a training program, most of which go well beyond the scope of this book. Although we may advocate that one drill be performed twice per week, if the skill is mastered easily a more complex variation can be attempted to maintain progress. The first 3 weeks of a mesocycle included in the speed, agility, and quickness program are dedicated to mastering specific skills. In the second 3 weeks of this mesocycle, we mix and match several drills to create more complex drills. Here is the time to get creative with your program. Feel free to change a drill or to combine it with a sport-specific skill or another drill. All of these drills were developed through experimentation. However, it is important to make sure that the athlete masters the basic movement patterns before taking on more complex drills or combining them with another skill. If a complex drill is done sloppily, it will do more harm than good by reinforcing poor movement patterns.

The training session format can be tailored to meet the specific needs and goals of the athlete or the team as a whole. Here is a good way to break it down:

1. A 3- to 5-minute session introduction that lays out the main goals of the session
2. A 10-minute warm-up
3. The body of the session: 20 to 25 sets of drills with a 1-to-3 or 1-to-4 work-to-rest ratio

4. Three or four 3-minute breaks for water, especially in hot climates

5. Always a cool-down that focuses on flexibility work.

Warm-Up

After the session introduction, begin preparing with a dynamic warm-up. As the drills of a particular session are mastered, they can eventually be used in the warm-up. Many of the drills in this book, such as skipping and carioca can serve as warm-up exercises. Using simple speed, agility, and quickness drills in the warm-up serves two main objectives. First, it prepares the body and CNS for work. Second, it teaches and reinforces proper biomotor skill execution without taking time away from the main goal of the training session. Over the course of a mesocycle, these 15- to 20-minute warm-ups can have a profound effect on biomotor skill acquisition and conditioning, ultimately adding up to several hours of work per mesocycle.

Use the following guidelines to ensure a safe and effective progression in the warm-up and during the entire training cycle. Perform each drill 2 to 4 times over 15 to 20 yards (14 to 18 meters), always moving from

1. simple to complex drills,
2. slow to fast execution speeds,
3. low- to high-intensity drills, and
4. lower to higher volume.

Below is a sample of a 15- to 20-minute warm-up using the drills in this book:

- A-March Walk
- B-March Walk
- Light jog
- Backpedal
- Skipping
- Backward Skipping
- Straight-Leg Shuffle
- Butt-Kickers
- Side-Shuffle
- Carioca
- Four-Point Pop-Up
- Single-Leg Balance With Opposite-Leg Reach
- Single-Leg Balance With Opposite-Arm Reach
- Multiplane Lunges

Body of the Session

The body of the session should emphasize an athlete's or group's major weaknesses or limiters. Don't feel as if you need to do an equal number of sets for each drill. If a particular drill proves challenging, focus on it instead of one that has been mastered. Provide appropriate rest between each drill. Remember that the major focus is to develop speed, agility, and quickness. This cannot take place in a fatigued state. A 1-to-3 or 1-to-4 work-to-rest ratio should provide ample recovery. However, if athletes are not well conditioned, they may need more time for recovery. In this case, lower the number of sets to be done per session and increase the rest periods. You'll get more out of the session with this approach. *More is not always better.*

When using speed, agility, and quickness training for conditioning, match the work-to-rest ratio of the target sport in order to make the training metabolically specific.

Because of individual differences, specific recommendations on the volume and intensity of exercises are impossible to make. However, ranges may be provided to serve as general guidelines. All exercises can be performed for the maximum number that can be accomplished in a specified period of time, usually between 5 and 10 seconds. Refer to chapter 1 for a fuller discussion of these variables.

Breaks and Cool-Down

Water breaks are a great way to provide rest and well-needed nourishment to the body, especially in hot climates. Keep water close by and provide a water break immediately after the warm-up, in the middle of the main body of the session, and at the end of the main body of the session (that is, right before flexibility work). Athletes are not always very conscientious about hydrating properly before a training session, so it's better for the coach to make sure they stay hydrated.

The cool-down, or flexibility session, is a time for gearing down, working on range-of-motion (ROM) issues using static flexibility exercises, and positively reflecting on the session. This session should not turn into a flexibility contest. Rather, it should focus on improving individual ROM deficits. Most stretching should be performed from a standing position so that gravity and ground reaction can load the muscles, joints, and connective tissues in a triplane environment consistent with what happens while competing and training.

Positive Reinforcement

Finish every session with positive affirmations. Focus on the successes of the session, not the failures. Speak of needed improvements in a positive manner and communicate an eagerness to accomplish your goals. No athlete likes to be reminded of or constantly badgered about his or her shortcomings. Athletes will respond better to a positive and respectful coaching style. Developing a good work ethic and desire to perform at the highest level possible begins with mutual respect and admiration between the coach and athlete.

Sample Sport-Specific Programs for Speed, Agility, and Quickness

The following pages list several examples of sport-specific speed, agility, and quickness programs. As stated above, when designing your own programs, it is important to focus on specificity of training and the needs of the athlete. One great way to improve specificity of training is to incorporate sport-specific tasks into your drills. For instance, programs for sports that require vertical jumping, like basketball and volleyball, should include vertical jumping drills. A football defensive back could catch a pass while performing reactive running drills. A creative mind and an understanding of the skills needed for each sport will ensure successful program design.

Tennis Sample Program

Goals: Improve serving power, change of direction, and reaction time.

Needs	WEEK 1 Drill name	Number	WEEK 2 Drill name	Number	WEEK 3 Drill name	Number
Speed	Ankling	2	A-Skip for distance (v)	7	A-Skip for height (v)	7
Speed	Wall Drills (Acceleration Marches)	24	Falling Starts	25	Heavy Sled Pulls	34
Agility	Icky Shuffle	82	Carioca	51	In-Out Shuffle	83
Agility	20-Yard Shuttle	53	30-Yard T-Drill	54	15-Yard Turn Drill	63
Quickness	Side-Shuffle	177	Lateral Skaters	137	Lateral Skaters to sprint	137
Quickness	Medicine-Ball Wall Scoop Toss	128	Medicine-Ball Wall Side Toss	126	Medicine-Ball Wall Overhead Throw	127

Needs	WEEK 4 Drill name	Number	WEEK 5 Drill name	Number	WEEK 6 Drill name	Number
Speed, agility, and quickness	Zigzag	68	Crossover Shuffle	85	Zigzag Crossover Shuffle	86
Speed, agility, and quickness	Lateral 20-Yard Shuttle (v)	53	Sprint and Cut on Command	169	Star Drill	171
Speed and quickness	Sprint to Medicine-Ball Wall Side Toss	126	Medicine-Ball Overhead Throw to sprint	127	Side-Shuffle to Medicine-Ball Side-to-Side Pass (v)	177, 126
Speed and quickness	V-Drill	78	Hop-Scotch Drill	150	V-Drill with ball drop (v)	78
Agility and quickness	Star Drill—Sprint, Backpedal, Shuffle	72	20-Yard Shuttle with ball pickup (v)	53	V-Drill while volleying (v)	78

Comments:

_____

_____

_____

_____

_____

_____

_____

(v) = variation

Note: Drills in weeks 4 through 6 should be performed on a tennis court using the court lines as markers. The court surface should be specific to what the player will be playing on.

Volleyball Sample Program

Goals: Defense—Increase vertical jump for blocks; improve reaction and level changes for digs; improve lateral quickness for digs. Offense—Improve vertical jump and core for spiking.

Needs	WEEK 1 Drill name	Number	WEEK 2 Drill name	Number	WEEK 3 Drill name	Number
Speed	Straight-Leg Shuffle	3	A-Skips	7	Skip for Height	40
Agility	Forward Roll Over Shoulder	96	Backward Roll Over Shoulder	97	Sprawl-to-Stand Pop-Up	175
Agility	Carioca	51	20-Yard Shuttle with carioca (v)	53	Star Drill—Sprint, Carioca, Backpedal	73
Quickness	In-Place Ankle Jumps	135	In-Place Tuck Jumps	138	Pike Jumps (v)	138
Quickness	Medicine-Ball Wall Chest Passes	124	Medicine-Ball Wall Chest Passes, single arm (v)	124	Medicine-Ball Bull in a Ring, single arm (v)	113

Needs	WEEK 4 Drill name	Number	WEEK 5 Drill name	Number	WEEK 6 Drill name	Number
Speed, agility, and quickness	Three-Step Foot Tap Drill With Sprint Plus Ball Drop	163	Side-Shuffle to bounce and catch (v)	177	Side-Shuffle to Sprawl-to-Stand Pop-Up	177, 175
Speed, agility, and quickness	Four-Point Pop-Up	172	Sit-to-Stand Pop-Up	173	Lying-to-Stand Pop-Up	174
Speed and quickness	Medicine-Ball Overhead Throw to sprint	127	Medicine-Ball Overhead Throw to Vertical Jump	127, 139	Medicine-Ball Overhead Throw to sprint	127
Speed and quickness	Repeated Vertical Jumps (v)	139	Side-Shuffle to Repeated Vertical Jumps	177, 139	Side-Shuffle to Ball Drops	177, 117
Agility and quickness	Backward Roll Over Shoulder to Vertical Jump	97, 139	Forward Roll Over Shoulder to Vertical Jump	96, 139	Sprawl-to-Stand Pop-Up to Vertical Jump	175, 139
Agility and quickness	Sprawl-to-Stand Pop-Up to H-Movement	175, 81	Lateral Skaters to bounce and catch (v)	137	Lateral Skaters to quick hands (v)	137

Comments:

_____
_____
_____
_____
_____
_____
_____
_____

(v) = variation

Boxing, Karate, and Tae Kwon Do Sample Program

Goals: Improve rotational power for punching and kicking; develop quickness for body positioning; develop quickness in hand and eye coordination and reaction.

Needs	WEEK 1 Drill name	Number	WEEK 2 Drill name	Number	WEEK 3 Drill name	Number
Speed	Skip for Height	40	Skip for Distance	41	Split-Squat Jumps	42
Speed	Stadium Stairs	32	Uphill Acceleration Run	33	Heavy Sled Pulls	34
Agility	Icky Shuffle	82	Carioca	51	In-Out Shuffle	83
Agility	Lateral Skaters	137	Hexagon Drill	104	Bag Hops With 180-Degree Turn	92
Quickness	Rope-Skipping	134	In-Place Ankle Jumps	135	Scissor Jumps	136
Quickness	The Bob	181	The Parry	182	The Weave	183

Needs	WEEK 4 Drill name	Number	WEEK 5 Drill name	Number	WEEK 6 Drill name	Number
Speed, agility, and quickness	Single-Leg Balance With Opposite-Leg Reach (3 planes)	106	Single-Leg Balance With Opposite-Arm Reach	107	Single-Leg Balance Dumbbell Presses	108
Speed, agility, and quickness	Snake Jump	87	180-Degree Turn	88	Lateral Skaters	137
Speed and quickness	Focus Mitt	184	Focus Mitt	184	The Bob to Focus Mitt	181, 184
Speed and quickness	The Bob to The Weave	181, 183	The Parry to The Weave	182, 183	The Weave to Focus Mitt	183, 184
Agility and quickness	Plyo Push-Ups	123	Medicine-Ball Wall Chest Passes	124	Medicine-Ball Wall Chest Passes, single arm (v)	124
Agility and quickness	Forward Roll Over Shoulder to Scissor Jumps	96, 136	Backward Roll Over Shoulder to Vertical Jump	97, 139	Cartwheel to Barrier Jumps	100, 141

Comments:

_____

_____

_____

_____

_____

_____

_____

(v) = variation

Wrestling and Judo Sample Program

Goals: Develop explosive power; improve powerful rotational mechanics for throws; increase agility from athletic position and quick reaction.

Needs	WEEK 1 Drill name	Number	WEEK 2 Drill name	Number	WEEK 3 Drill name	Number
Speed	A-Skips	7	A-Form Runs (v)	7	Sand Running	18
	Stadium Stairs	32	Uphill Acceleration Run	33	Heavy Sled Pulls	34
Agility	Forward Roll–Backward Roll Combination	99	Sprawl-to-Stand Pop-Up	175	Sprawl, Roll, and Stand Up (v)	175
	Snake Jump	87	180-Degree Turn	88	Bag Hops With 180-Degree Turn	92
Quickness	Wheelbarrow	122	Stability-Ball Hops	121	Medicine-Ball Lateral Shuffle/Pass	114
	Weighted Rope-Skipping (v)	134	In-Place Tuck Jumps	138	Repeated Pike Jumps (v)	138

Needs	WEEK 4 Drill name	Number	WEEK 5 Drill name	Number	WEEK 6 Drill name	Number
Speed, agility, and quickness	Dodge Ball	185	Dodge Ball to Sprawl-to-Stand Pop-Up	185, 175	Dodge Ball to In-Place Tuck Jumps	185, 138
	The Bob	181	The Parry	182	The Weave	183
Speed and quickness	Medicine-Ball Wall Side Toss	126	Medicine-Ball Overhead Throw	127	Medicine-Ball Reverse Scoop Toss (v)	128
	Repeated Vertical Jumps (v)	139	Split-Squat Jumps	42	Alternating Split-Squat Jumps (v)	42
Agility and quickness	Directional Hand Movement	166	Directional Mirror Drill	167	Side-to-Side Skiers	94
	Sprawl-to-Stand Pop-Up to Medicine-Ball Lateral Shuffle/Pass	175, 114	Sprawl-to-Stand Pop-Up to Vertical Jump	175, 139	Sprawl-to-Stand Pop-Up to Barrier Jumps	175, 141

Comments:

_____

_____

_____

_____

_____

_____

_____

(v) = variation

Baseball, Softball, and Cricket (Infielders) Sample Program

Goals: Improve quick response and lateral movement for throwing speed and fielding range; improve acceleration and turning ability for faster base running; increase bat speed.

Needs	WEEK 1 Drill name	Number	WEEK 2 Drill name	Number	WEEK 3 Drill name	Number
Speed	A-Skips	7	Light Sled/Tire Pulls	15	Parachute Running	17
Speed	Wall Drills (Acceleration Marches)	24	Acceleration Runs	30	Uphill Acceleration Run	33
Agility	20-Yard Shuttle	53	Figure Eights	66	Z-Pattern Run	67
Agility	Zigzag	68	Crossover Shuffle	85	Zigzag Crossover Shuffle	86
Quickness	Ball Drops With a Partner	117	Partner Blind Tosses	119	Goalie Drill	118
Quickness	Medicine-Ball Overhead Throw	127	Medicine-Ball Wall Side Toss	126	Medicine-Ball Side-to-Side (v)	126

Needs	WEEK 4 Drill name	Number	WEEK 5 Drill name	Number	WEEK 6 Drill name	Number
Speed, agility, and quickness	Side-to-Side Skiers With Front Rotation	95	Side-to-Side Skiers With Front Rotation	95	Side-to-Side With Back Rotation (v)	95
Speed, agility, and quickness	15-Yard Turn Drill	63	20-Yard Square	64	30-Yard Square (v)	64
Speed and quickness	Side-Shuffle	177	Backpedal	111	Sprint and Cut on Command	169
Speed and quickness	Sprint to Medicine-Ball Overhead Throw	127	Sprint to Medicine-Ball Wall Side Toss	126	Medicine-Ball Wall Side Toss to sprint	126
Agility and quickness	180-Degree Turn	88	Snake Jump	87	Lateral Skaters	137
Agility and quickness	Icky Shuffle while fielding ball (v)	82	Crossover Shuffle while fielding ball (v)	85	Half-Ladder Skill to pick up ball (v)	152

Comments:

_____

_____

_____

_____

_____

_____

_____

(v) = variation

Football (Running Back) and Rugby (Forward) Sample Program

Goals: Develop first-step quickness; increase acceleration; train change of direction.

Needs	WEEK 1 Drill name	Number	WEEK 2 Drill name	Number	WEEK 3 Drill name	Number
Speed	Straight-Leg Shuffle	3	Single-Leg Run-Through	12	Run-Through	13
	Wall Drills (Acceleration Marches)	24	Uphill Acceleration Run	33	Heavy Sled Pulls	34
Agility	Four-Point Pop-Up	172	Squirm	55	Squirm	55
	15-Yard Turn Drill	63	Z-Pattern Cuts	69	V-Drill	78
Quickness	Plyo Push-Ups	123	Stability-Ball Cyclic Impact Lockouts	120	Stability-Ball Hops	121
	Medicine-Ball Wall Chest Passes	124	Medicine-Ball Wall Chest Passes, single arm (v)	124	Medicine-Ball Lateral Shuffle/Pass	114

Needs	WEEK 4 Drill name	Number	WEEK 5 Drill name	Number	WEEK 6 Drill name	Number
Speed, agility, and quickness	Star Drill—Sprint, Backpedal, Shuffle	72	Star Drill—Sprint, Carioca, Backpedal	73	Star Drill—Sprint, Bear Crawl, Shuffle	74
	Bag Weave	89	Lateral Weave	91	Bag Hops With 180-Degree Turn	92
Speed and quickness	Medicine-Ball Lateral Shuffle/Pass to sprint	114	Sprint to Medicine-Ball Lateral Shuffle/Pass	114	Sprint to Plyo Push-Ups	123
	Medicine-Ball Wall Scoop Toss	128	Medicine-Ball Squat, Push Toss, Bounce, and Catch	115	Medicine-Ball Forward Scoop Toss, Bounce, and Catch	116
Agility and quickness	Forward Roll Over Shoulder to ball catch (v)	96	Sprint to Forward Roll Over Shoulder	96	Running Start and Tumbling Over Barrier (v)	102
	Four-Point Pop-Up to ball catch (v)	172	Sprawl-to-Stand Pop-Up to ball catch (v)	175	Sprawl-to-Stand Pop-Up to sprint (v)	175

Comments:

_____

_____

_____

_____

_____

_____

_____

(v) = variation

Basketball and Netball Sample Program

Goals: Defense—Improve jumping ability for rebounding and blocking; improve lateral mobility for coverage and change of direction. Offense—Improve jumping ability for shooting; improve first-step quickness and acceleration for breakaways.

Needs	WEEK 1 Drill name	Number	WEEK 2 Drill name	Number	WEEK 3 Drill name	Number
Speed	A-March Walk	6	A-Skips for distance (v)	7	A-Skips for height (v)	7
	A-Form Runs (v)	7	Partner-Resisted Starts	35	Bullet Belt	39
Agility	20-Yard Shuttle	53	Lateral 20-Yard Shuttle (v)	53	30-Yard T-Drill	54
	Medicine-Ball Wall Chest Passes	124	Medicine-Ball Overhead Throw	127	Medicine-Ball Wall Scoop Toss	128
Quickness	Repeated Vertical Jumps (v)	139	Standing Long Jump	140	Power Skips	142

Needs	WEEK 4 Drill name	Number	WEEK 5 Drill name	Number	WEEK 6 Drill name	Number
Speed, agility, and quickness	Squirm	55	X-Pattern Multiskill	65	Z-Pattern Cuts	69
	Hexagon Drill	104	Hexagon Drill	104	Drop and Get Up	103
Speed and quickness	Ladder Speed Runs	10	Hop-Scotch Drill to catch a pass (v)	150	One-Leg Hop to dribble and lay-up (v)	151
	Repeated Vertical Jumps (v)	139	Vertical Jump to sprint	139	Sprint to Vertical Jump	139
Agility and quickness	Backward Icky Shuffle	192	Medicine-Ball Lateral Shuffle/Pass	114	Medicine-Ball Lateral Shuffle/ Pass, with one partner leading (v)	114
	Four-Point Pop-Up to 20-Yard Shuttle	172	Sit-to-Stand Pop-Up to Z-Pattern Run	173, 167	Lying-to-Stand Pop-Up to 30-Yard T-Drill	174, 54

Comments:

_____

_____

_____

_____

_____

_____

_____

(v) = variation

Soccer and Lacrosse Sample Program

Goals: Improve lateral agility and quickness; train level changes during slide tackles; increase open field acceleration.

Needs	WEEK 1 Drill name	Number	WEEK 2 Drill name	Number	WEEK 3 Drill name	Number
Speed	Single-Leg Run-Through	12	Run-Through	13	Run-Through alternating fast legs (v)	13
	Gears	28	Uphill Speed Runs	16	Uphill-to-Flat Contrast Speed Runs	20
Agility	Figure Eights	66	Z-Pattern Run	67	Z-Pattern Cuts	69
	Four-Point Pop-Up	172	Sprawl-to-Stand Pop-Up	175	Sprawl, Roll, and Stand Up (v)	175
Quickness	Hop-Scotch to reaction sprint (v)	190	Quick Feet to reaction sprint (v)	148	Half Ladder Skill to reaction sprint (v)	152
	Repeated Vertical Jumps	139	Lateral Skaters	137	Vertical Jump to sprint	139

Needs	WEEK 4 Drill name	Number	WEEK 5 Drill name	Number	WEEK 6 Drill name	Number
Speed, agility, and quickness	Four-Point Pop-Up to 20-Yard Shuttle	172, 53	Sprawl-to-Stand Pop-Up to Squirm	175, 55	Forward Roll–Backward Roll Combination to Squirm	99, 55
	Forward Roll Over Shoulder	96	Backward Roll Over Shoulder	97	Cartwheel	100
Speed and quickness	Medicine-Ball Overhead Throw	127	Medicine-Ball Wall Scoop Toss	128	Medicine-Ball Squat, Push Toss, Bounce, and Catch	115
	Lateral Skaters	137	Repeated Vertical Jumps (v)	139	Sprint to Vertical Jump	139
Agility and quickness	Half Ladder Skill to ball control (v)	152	Half Ladder Skill to shoot (v)	152	Half Ladder Skill to trap and shoot (v)	152
	Sprint and Backpedal on Command	168	Sprint and Cut on Command	169	Star Drill	171

Comments:
_____
_____
_____
_____
_____
_____
_____

(v) = variation

Customizable Sample Program Template
Goals:

Needs	WEEK 1		WEEK 2		WEEK 3	
	Drill name	Number	Drill name	Number	Drill name	Number
Speed						
Agility						
Quickness						

Needs	WEEK 4		WEEK 5		WEEK 6	
	Drill name	Number	Drill name	Number	Drill name	Number
Speed, agility, and quickness						
Speed and quickness						
Agility and quickness						

Comments:
_____
_____
_____
_____
_____
_____
_____

From *Training for Speed, Agility, and Quickness, Second Edition,* edited by Lee E. Brown and Vance A. Ferrigno, 2005, Champaign, IL: Human Kinetics.

References

Chapter 2

Aján, T., and L. Baroga. 1988. *Weightlifting.* Budapest: International Weightlifting Federation/ Medicina.

Dick, F.W. 1987. *Sprints and relays.* London: British Amateur Athletic Board.

Field, R.W. 1989. Control tests for explosive events. *National Strength and Conditioning Association Journal* 11(6): 63-64.

———. 1991. Explosive power test scores among male and female college athletes. *National Strength and Conditioning Association Journal* 13(3): 50.

Garstecki, M.A., R.W. Latin, and M.M. Cuppett. 2004. Comparison of selected physical fitness and performance variables between NCAA Division I and II football players. *Journal of Strength and Conditioning Research* 18(2): 292-297.

Plisk, S.S. 1994. Regression analyses of NCAA Division I Final Four men's lacrosse competition. *Journal of Strength and Conditioning Research* 8(1): 28-42.

———. 2000a. Speed, agility, and speed-endurance development. In *Essentials of strength training and conditioning*, 2d ed., ed. T.R. Baechle, R.W. Earle, and National Strength and Conditioning Association, 471-491. Champaign IL: Human Kinetics.

———. 2000b. The angle on agility. *Training and Conditioning* 10(6): 37-43.

Plisk, S.S., and V. Gambetta. 1997. Tactical metabolic training. *Strength and Conditioning* 19(2): 44-53.

Plisk, S.S., and S.B. Stenersen. 1992. The lacrosse face-off. *National Strength and Conditioning Association Journal* 14(2): 6-8 and 77-91.

Schmidtbleicher, D. 1985a. Strength training (part 1): Classification of methods. *Science Periodical on Research and Technology in Sport* (Physical Training/Strength W-4) (August): 1-12.

———. 1985b. Strength training (part 2): Structural analysis of motor strength qualities and its application to training. *Science Periodical on Research and Technology in Sport* (Physical Training/Strength W-4) (September): 1-10.

———. 1992. Training for power events. In *Strength and power in sport*, ed. P.V. Komi, 381-395. Oxford: Blackwell Scientific.

Schmolinsky, G. (ed.). 1993. *Track and field.* Toronto: Sport Books.

Secora, C.A., R.W. Latin, K.E. Berg, and J.M. Noble. 2004. Comparison of physical and performance characteristics of NCAA Division I football players: 1987 and 2000. *Journal of Strength and Conditioning Research* 18(2): 286-291.

Siff, M.C. 2003. *Supertraining.* 6th ed. Denver: Supertraining Institute.

Steinhofer, D. 1997. Terminology and differentiation of training methods. *Modern Athlete and Coach* 35(1): 15-21.

Taylor, J. 2003. Basketball: Applying time motion data to conditioning. *Strength and Conditioning Journal* 25(2): 57-64.

———. 2004. A tactical metabolic training model for collegiate basketball. *Strength and Conditioning Journal* 26(5): 22-29.

Zatsiorsky, V.M. 1995. *Science and practice of strength training.* Champaign IL: Human Kinetics.

Chapter 4

Arthur, M., and B. Bailey. 1998. *Complete conditioning for football.* Champaign, IL: Human Kinetics.

Barnes, M., and J. Attaway. 1996. Agility and conditioning of the San Francisco 49ers. *Strength and Conditioning* 18(4): 10-16.

Bates, B.T. 1970. The relationships of performance on lateral change of direction agility tests. Master's thesis. *Health, Physical Education, and Recreation* (microfiche publication). East Stroudsburg State College, East Stroudsburg, PA.

Brant, J.J., and B.W. Findley. 2001. Postrehabilitation balance training for the strength and conditioning professional. *Strength and Conditioning* 23(5): 55-59.

Brittenham, G. 1996. *Complete conditioning for basketball.* Champaign, IL: Human Kinetics.

Chipps, E., N. Clanin, and V. Campbell. 1992. *Neurologic disorders.* St. Louis: Mosby.

Cissik, J., and M. Barnes. 2004. *Sport speed and agility.* Monterey, CA: Coaches Choice.

Cohen, S.B., W.C. Whiting, and A.J. McLaine. 2002. Implementation of balance training in a gymnast's conditioning program. *Strength and Conditioning* 24(2): 60-67.

Costello, F., and E.J. Kreis. 1993. *Sports agility.* Nashville, TN: Taylor Sports.

Fleck, S.J., and W.J. Kraemer. 1997. *Designing resistance programs.* 2d ed. Champaign, IL: Human Kinetics.

Gambetta, V., and S. Myrland. 1998. *Speed/agility: Ladder footwork drills.* Videocassette. Sarasota, FL: Gambetta Sports Training Systems.

Gray, G. 2004. *Functional video digest series: Balance,* 1.6. Videocassette. Adrian, MI: Functional Design Systems.

———. 2001. *Total body functional profile.* Adrian, MI: Wynn Marketing.

———. 2001. *3D Dumbbell Matrix Video.* Videocassette. Adrian, MI: Functional Design Systems.

Halberg, G.V. 2001. Relationships among power, acceleration, maximum speed, programmed agility, and reactive agility: The neural fundamentals of agility. Masters thesis. Central Michigan University, Mount Pleasant, MI.

Harman, E. 2000. The biomechanics of resistance exercise. In *Essentials of strength training and conditioning,* 2d ed., ed. T.R. Baechle, R.W. Earle, and National Strength and Conditioning Association. Champaign, IL: Human Kinetics.

Holcomb, W. 2000. Stretching and warm-up. In *Essentials of strength training and conditioning,* 2d ed., ed. T.R. Baechle, R.W. Earle, and National Strength and Conditioning Association. Champaign, IL: Human Kinetics.

Knuttgen, H., and W. Kraemer. 1987. Terminology and measurement in exercise performance. *Journal of Applied Sport Science Research* 1(1): 1-10.

Murphy, P., and J. Forney. 1997. *Complete conditioning for baseball.* Champaign, IL: Human Kinetics.

Plisk, S. 2000. Speed, agility, and speed-endurance development. In *Essentials of strength training and conditioning,* 2d ed., ed. T.R. Baechle, R.W. Earle, and National Strength and Conditioning Association. Champaign, IL: Human Kinetics.

Santana, J.C. 2002. Sports-specific conditioning: Stability and balance training: Performance training or circus acts? *Strength and Conditioning* 24(4): 76-77.

Siff, M. 2000. *Fitness Facts and Fallacies.* Denver, CO.

Verstegen, M. 2004. *Core performance.* Emmaus, PA: Rodale.

Chapter 5

Clark, M. 2001. *Integrated training for the new millennium.* Thousand Oaks, CA: National Academy of Sports Medicine.

Enoka, R.M. 1997. Neural adaptations with chronic physical activity. *Journal of Biomechanics* 30: 447-455.

Green, M. 1999. "How long does it take to stop?" Methodological analysis of driver perception-brake times. *Transportation Human Factors* 2(3), 195-216.

Guyton, A.C. 1991. *Textbook of medical physiology.* 6th ed. Philadelphia: Sanders.

Hick, W.E. 1952. On the rate of gain of information. *Quarterly Journal of Experimental Psychology* 4: 1-26.

Hodgson, J., R. Roy, R. DeLeon, et al. 1994. Can the mammalian lumbar spinal cord learn a motor task? *Medicine and Science in Sports and Exercise* 26: 1491-1497.

Jeeves, M.A. 1961. Changes in performance at a serial reaction task under conditions of advance and delay of information. *Ergonomics* 4: 329-338.

Laming, D.R.J. 1968. *Information theory of choice-reaction times.* London: Academic Press.

Leonard, J.A. 1953. Advance information in sensori-motor skills. *Quarterly Journal of Experimental Psychology* 5: 141-149.

———. 1954. An experiment with occasional false information. *Quarterly Journal of Experimental Psychology* 11: 79-85.

Liston, J., and R. dos Remedios. 2003. Developing sport-speed using "open" agility and quickness drills. Presentation handout. 2003 Annual Sport Specific Conference. National Strength and Conditioning Association.

Nickerson, R.S. 1972. Binary-classification reaction times: A review of some studies of human information-processing capabilities. *Psychonomic Monograph Supplements* 4: 275-318.

Posner, M.I., M.J. Nissen, and W.C. Ogden. 1978. Attended and unattended processing modes: The role of set for spatial location. In *Modes of perceiving and processing information,* ed. H.L Pick and I.J. Saltzman, 137-157. Hillsdale, NJ: Erlbaum.

Prentice, W.E., and M.I. Voight. 1999. *Techniques in musculoskeletal rehabilitation.* Chicago: McGraw-Hill.

Schmidt, R.A., and G.B. Gordon. 1977. Errors in motor responding, "rapid" corrections, and false anticipations. *Journal of Motor Behavior* 9: 101-111.

Schmidt, R.A., and T.D. Lee. 1998. *Motor control and learning: A behavioral emphasis.* 3d ed. Champaign, IL: Human Kinetics.

Schmidt, R.A., and C.A. Wrisberg. 2000. *Motor learning and performance.* 2d ed. Champaign, IL: Human Kinetics.

Zatsiorsky, V. 1995. *Science and practice of strength training.* Champaign, IL: Human Kinetics.

Chapter 6

Brown, L.E., and R.H. Knee. 1999. Monitoring periodization with a spreadsheet. *Strength and Conditioning* 21(6): 45-49.

Brown, L.E., and J.P. Weir. 2001. ASEP procedures recommendations for the accurate assessment of muscular strength and power. *Journal of Exercise Physiology* (online) 4(3): 1-21.

Miller, J.M., S.C. Hilbert, and L.E. Brown. 2001. Speed, agility, and quickness training for senior tennis players. *Strength and Conditioning* 23(5): 62-66.

Yap, C.W., L.E. Brown, and G. Woodman. 2000. Development of speed, agility and quickness for the female soccer athlete. *Strength and Conditioning* 22(1): 9-12, 2000.

Drill Finder

Name	Drill #	Page #	Emphasis	Level	Equipment	Shown on DVD
SPEED						
Acceleration Runs (17- and 4-Inch)	30	51	Acceleration Top-end running Proper striding	Intermediate	Acceleration ladder or sticks	●
A-March Walk	6	28	Foot speed	Basic		
Ankling	2	24	Foot speed Ankle strength	Intermediate		
A-Skips	7	29	Hip extension Flexion strength Ankle-muscle stiffness	Intermediate		
Basic 40-Yard Model	27	48	Starting, acceleration, and maximum-speed integration	Intermediate		
B-March Walk	8	30	Hip extension Hamstring firing	Intermediate		
Bounding	43	64	Hip extension and flexion strength Ankle-muscle stiffness Leg power Stride length	Advanced		●
B-Skips	9	31	Stride length and frequency Hamstring and hip performance Ankle-muscle stiffness	Intermediate		
Bullet Belt	39	60	Quick transitions in speed Stride frequency	Intermediate	Bullet belt	
Butt-Kickers	4	26	Foot speed	Basic		●
Contrast Parachute Running	19	40	Stride length of start Turnover at top speed Starting speed Transition to top speed	Intermediate	Small parachute attached to a belt	
Contrast Sled/Tire Pulls	21	42	Stride length of start Turnover at top speed Starting speed Transition to top speed	Advanced	Weighted sled or tire attached to a belt	
Downhill Speed Runs (3- to 7-Degree Decline)	22	43	Top-end speed Stride frequency	Advanced		●
Downhill-to-Flat Contrast Speed Runs (3- to 5-Degree Decline)	23	44	Top-end speed Stride frequency	Advanced		●
Falling Starts	25	46	Quick leg turnover Acceleration lean	Basic		●

Name	Drill #	Page #	Emphasis	Level	Equipment	Shown on DVD
4 × 4s	46	67	Hip flexor range of motion Stride length	Basic		
Galloping	48	69	Hip projection Back leg push-off Lead-leg mechanics Pawing mechanics	Intermediate		
Gears	28	49	Transition acceleration Changing speeds	Intermediate	Cones	
Harness Pull	37	58	Acceleration	Intermediate	Harness	
Heavy Sled Pulls	34	55	Starting power Stride length	Advanced	Weighted sled or tire attached to a belt	
Heel and Toe Walks	47	68	Dorsiflexed foot position Shin splints prevention	Basic		
High Knees	45	66	"Thigh-parallel-to-the-ground" technique	Basic		
Hurdle Fast Legs	14	36	Stride frequency Hip flexor strength Lower-body ambidexterity	Advanced	6- to 12-inch hurdles	●
Ins and Outs	29	50	Transition acceleration Changing speeds	Intermediate	Cones	
Ladder Speed Run	10	32	Timing Stride frequency Quick turnover	Intermediate	Agility ladder or sticks	●
Ladder Stride Run	11	33	Timing Stride frequency Quick turnover	Intermediate	Agility ladder or sticks	●
Light Sled/Tire Pulls	15	37	Running strength and power Stride length	Intermediate	Weighted sled or tire attached to a belt	●
Moye (Crouched-Variation) Starts	26	47	Reaction time Starting response First-step quickness Acceleration mechanics	Basic		
Parachute Running	17	39	Running strength and power Stride length	Intermediate	Small parachute attached to a belt	
Partner-Assisted Let-Gos	38	59	Quick transitions in speed Stride frequency	Basic	Towel or rope (optional)	●
Partner-Resisted Starts	35	56	Starting power Stride length	Basic	Towel (optional)	●
Partner Tubing-Assisted Acceleration Drill	36	57	Quick leg recovery Stride frequency	Advanced	10- to 20-yard rubber tubing	●

Name	Drill #	Page #	Emphasis	Level	Equipment	Shown on DVD
Pit Smashers	50	70	Driving out of blocks Hip, knee, and ankle extension	Advanced	High-jump pit or sand (long-jump) pit	
Pool Drills	49	70	Recovery	Basic	Swimming pool	
Run-Through	13	35	Stride frequency Hip flexor strength Lower-body ambidexterity	Intermediate	6- to 12-inch hurdles	◉
Sand Running	18	40	Stride length Hip strength	Intermediate		
Single-Leg Bounds	44	65	Hip extension and flexion strength Ankle-muscle stiffness Leg power Stride length	Advanced		
Single-Leg Run-Through	12	34	Stride frequency Hip flexor strength Lower-body ambidexterity	Intermediate	6- to 12-inch hurdles	◉
Skip for Distance	41	62	Hip power Stride length	Advanced		◉
Skip for Height	40	61	Hip extension and flexion strength Ankle-muscle stiffness Leg power Stride length	Advanced		◉
Split-Squat Jumps	42	63	Hip power Stride length	Advanced		
Stadium Stairs	32	53	Starting power Stride length	Intermediate		
Standing Stationary Arm Swings	1	23	Running mechanics	Basic		
Straight-Leg Shuffle	3	25	Hip strength Ankle strength	Advanced		
Uphill Acceleration Run	33	54	Starting power Stride length	Advanced		
Uphill Speed Runs (1- to 3-Degree Incline)	16	38	Running strength and power Stride length	Advanced		◉
Uphill-to-Flat Contrast Speed Runs (15- to 20-Degree Incline)	20	41	Stride length of start Turnover at top speed Starting speed Transition to top speed	Advanced		
Wall Drills (Acceleration Marches)	24	45	Ankle-muscle stiffness Lower-body elastic strength	Basic		
Wall Slides	5	27	Knee lift Turnover frequency	Basic		
Weighted Starts	31	52	Elastic strength at start	Intermediate	Weighted vest or shot belt	

Name	Drill #	Page #	Emphasis	Level	Equipment	Shown on DVD
AGILITY						
A-Movement	79	105	Changing direction Body position Transitions between skills Cutting	Interme-diate	Cones	●
Backward Roll Over Shoulder	97	122	Total-body agility Kinesthetic awareness	Advanced		●
Backward Roll to Hand Push-Off	98	123	Total-body agility Kinesthetic awareness	Advanced		
Bag Hops With 180-Degree Turn	92	118	Foot quickness Hip flexibility	Advanced	Bags	
Bag Weave	89	115	Flexibility High-knee action Foot quickness	Interme-diate	Bags	
Carioca	51	77	Balance Hip flexibility Footwork Lateral speed	Interme-diate		
Cartwheel	100	125	Total-body agility Kinesthetic awareness	Interme-diate		
Combo Sidestep/ Forward-Back	90	116	Changing direction Flexibility High-knee action Foot quickness	Advanced	Bags	
Crossover Shuffle	85	111	Hip flexibility and power Changing direction	Interme-diate	Agility ladder	
Crossover Skipping	52	78	Explosive crossover mechanics Explosive contralateral hip flexion and extension	Advanced		
Drop and Get Up	103	128	Changing direction Reaction time	Interme-diate	Crazy Z-ball	●
E-Movement	80	106	Changing direction Body position Transitions between skills Cutting	Interme-diate	Cones	
15-Yard Turn Drill	63	89	Changing direction Hip flexibility Footwork	Interme-diate	Cones	
55-Yard Sprint-Backpedal	60	86	Acceleration Stopping ability	Advanced	Marked lines	●
Figure Eights	66	92	Changing direction Reaction time	Basic	Cones	●
Five-Cone Snake Drill	75	101	Changing direction Body position Transitions between skills Cutting	Interme-diate	Cones	●
40-Yard Backpedal-Forward	59	85	Agility Changing direction Conditioning	Advanced	Marked lines	●

Name	Drill #	Page #	Emphasis	Level	Equipment	Shown on DVD
40-Yard Lateral Shuffle	58	84	Agility, conditioning, and flexibility in abductors and adductors Strength	Intermediate	Marked lines	
40-Yard Sprint	56	82	Agility Conditioning	Intermediate	Marked lines	
40-Yard Square—Carioca	62	88	Changing direction Hip flexibility Footwork	Intermediate	Cones	
40-Yard Square Drill—Sprint, Bear Crawl, Backpedal	70	96	Changing direction Body position Transitions between skills Cutting	Advanced	Cones	
40-Yard Square Drill—Sprint, Single-Leg Hop, Backpedal	71	97	Changing direction Body position Transitions between skills Cutting	Advanced	Cones	
Forward Roll–Backward Roll Combination	99	124	Total-body agility Kinesthetic awareness	Advanced		
Forward Roll Over Shoulder	96	121	Total-body agility Kinesthetic awareness	Basic		
Hexagon Drill	104	129	Agility	Basic	Marked lines	
H-Movement	81	107	Changing direction Body position Transitions between skills Cutting	Intermediate	Cones	
Icky Shuffle	82	108	Coordination Lower-body quickness	Intermediate	Agility ladder	
In-Out Shuffle	83	109	Agility Balance Coordination Quickness	Basic	Agility ladder	
Lateral Weave	91	117	Foot quickness Reaction time	Intermediate	Bags	
180-Degree Turn	88	114	Agility Balance Hip flexibility Quickness	Intermediate	Agility ladder	
100-Yard Sprint	61	87	Changing direction Footwork Reaction time	Advanced	Marked lines	
Round-Off	101	126	Total-body agility Kinesthetic awareness	Intermediate		
S-Drill	76	102	Changing direction Body position Transitions between skills Cutting	Intermediate	Cones	
Side Right-In	84	110	Agility Balance Coordination Quickness	Intermediate	Agility ladder	

Name	Drill #	Page #	Emphasis	Level	Equipment	Shown on DVD
Side-to-Side Skiers	94	119	Agility Rotational change of direction	Advanced	Angle board	
Side-to-Side Skiers With Front Rotation	95	120	Lateral agility Rotational transition Balance	Advanced	Slide board	
60-Yard Shuttle Sprint	57	83	Agility Conditioning	Intermediate	Marked lines	
Snake Jump	87	113	Agility Balance Coordination Hip flexibility Quickness	Intermediate	Agility ladder	
Squirm	55	81	Footwork Reaction time	Intermediate		
Star Drill—Sprint, Backpedal, Shuffle	72	98	Changing direction Body position Transitions between skills Cutting	Advanced	Cones	
Star Drill—Sprint, Bear Crawl, Shuffle	74	100	Changing direction Body position Transitions between skills Cutting	Advanced	Cones	
Star Drill—Sprint, Carioca, Backpedal	73	99	Changing direction Body position Transitions between skills Cutting	Advanced	Cones	
10-Cone Snake Drill	77	103	Changing direction Body position Transitions between skills Cutting	Intermediate	Cones	
30-Yard T-Drill	54	80	Agility, conditioning, and flexibility in abductors and adductors Strength	Intermediate	Marked lines	
Toss, Get Up, and Catch	105	130	Level changing Transition from power to agility	Intermediate	Medicine ball	
Tumbling Drill Variations	102	127	Total-body agility Kinesthetic awareness	Basic	Barrier	
20-Yard Shuttle	53	79	Changing direction Footwork Reaction time	Basic	Marked lines	
20-Yard Square	64	90	Changing direction Body position Transitions between skills Cutting	Intermediate	Cones	
V-Drill	78	104	Changing direction Body position Transitions between skills Cutting	Basic	Cones	
Wheel	93	118	Balance Foot quickness	Basic	Bags	

Name	Drill #	Page #	Emphasis	Level	Equipment	Shown on DVD
X-Pattern Multiskill	65	91	Transitional movement Cutting	Advanced	Cones	●
Zigzag	68	94	Footwork Quickness	Intermediate	Cones	
Zigzag Crossover Shuffle	86	112	Abductor and adductor flexibility Footwork Changing direction	Advanced	Agility ladder	●
Z-Pattern Cuts	69	95	Cutting	Advanced	Cones	
Z-Pattern Run	67	93	Transitional movement Turning	Intermediate	Cones	●
BALANCE						
Hop-and-Stick Balance Drills	109	134	Balance in dynamic situations	Basic		●
Single-Leg Balance With Opposite-Arm Reach	107	132	Single-leg balance	Intermediate		●
Single-Leg Balance With Opposite-Leg Reach	106	131	Single-leg balance	Intermediate		●
Lunge Patterns	110	135	Lower-limb strength	Intermediate		●
Single-Leg Balance Dumbbell Presses	108	133	Single-leg balance with resistance	Advanced	Dumbbells	●
QUICKNESS						
Backpedal	111	144	Hip flexor quickness and flexibility	Intermediate		
Ball Drops With a Partner	117	150	Visual stimulus response First-step quickness	Basic	Sports ball	
Barrier Jumps	141	173	Lower-body power and quickness	Advanced	Hurdle, box, or cones	
Barrier Jump With Cut and Sprint	144	176	Lower-body power and quickness	Advanced	Hurdle or bag, cones	●
Bunny Jumps	149	181	Ankle elastic strength	Basic	Agility ladder	
Containing-Opponent Drill	157	189	Changing direction Reaction	Basic	Marked lines or cones	●
Explosive Reclined Pulls	133	165	Power and quickness in upper-body pulling musculature	Advanced	Rope and bar or hook	
Goalie Drill	118	151	Upper-body quickness	Intermediate	Sports ball, cones, marked line	
Half Ladder Skill to Sport-Specific Skill	152	184	Lower-body quickness	Advanced	Agility ladder, sports ball	
Hop-Scotch Drill	150	182	Ankle elastic strength	Basic	Agility ladder	
In-Place Ankle Jumps	135	167	Lower-body quickness and elastic strength	Basic		
In-Place Tuck Jumps	138	170	Lower-body power	Advanced		
Jump Rope With Multidirectional Jumps	146	178	Lower-body power and quickness	Intermediate	Jump rope	

Name	Drill #	Page #	Emphasis	Level	Equipment	Shown on DVD
Lateral Skaters	137	169	Cutting First-step lateral quickness	Interme-diate		
Lunge With Power-Up Jump	143	175	Lower-body power and quickness	Advanced		◉
Medicine-Ball Bull in a Ring	113	146	Quickness Elastic strength	Interme-diate	Medicine ball	
Medicine-Ball Forward Scoop Toss, Bounce, and Catch	116	149	Total-body power Reactive strength	Advanced	Medicine ball	◉
Medicine-Ball Lateral Shuffle/Pass	114	147	Quickness Elastic strength	Interme-diate	Medicine ball	
Medicine-Ball One-Arm Push-Off	130	163	Power and quickness in upper-body pushing musculature	Advanced	Medicine ball	
Medicine-Ball Overhead Throw	127	160	Explosive power in throwing and overhead activities	Interme-diate	Medicine ball	◉
Medicine-Ball Release Push-Ups With Partner	125	158	Quickness in upper-body pushing musculature	Advanced	Medicine ball	◉
Medicine-Ball Squat, Push Toss, Bounce, and Catch	115	148	Reactive elastic strength Total-body power	Advanced	Medicine ball	
Medicine-Ball Upper-Body Shuffles	131	164	Power and quickness in upper-body pushing musculature	Interme-diate	Medicine ball	◉
Medicine-Ball Wall Chest Passes	124	157	Total-body transmission of power	Interme-diate	Medicine ball	◉
Medicine-Ball Wall Scoop Toss	128	161	Total-body extension, quickness, and power	Interme-diate	Medicine ball	
Medicine-Ball Wall Side Toss	126	159	Explosive rotational mechanics Changing direction	Interme-diate	Medicine ball	◉
Mirror Drills in Box With Square Shuffle	159	191	Lower-body lateral quickness Reaction	Interme-diate	Cones	
Mirroring Partner Sprints	156	188	Changing direction	Basic	Marked lines or cones	◉
Mirroring Two-Box Drill	158	190	Changing direction Reaction	Basic	Cones	◉
Mirror Two-Box Drill With Switching Commander	164	195	Total-body quickness Changing direction	Interme-diate	Cones	
Multidirectional Skipping	112	145	Quickness Coordination	Advanced		
One-Leg Hop	151	183	Lower-body quickness	Interme-diate	Agility ladder	
Partner Blind Tosses	119	152	Upper- and lower-body quickness and reaction	Advanced	Tennis ball or Crazy Z-ball	◉
Partner-Resisted Lateral Shuffle and Chase	155	187	Lower-body quickness and reaction Changing direction	Advanced		◉
Plyo Push-Ups	123	156	Quickness in upper-body pushing musculature	Advanced		
Power Skips	142	174	Lower-body power and quickness	Advanced		

Name	Drill #	Page #	Emphasis	Level	Equipment	Shown on DVD
Push-Off Box Shuffle	145	177	Lower-body power and quickness	Intermediate	Box or step	●
Quick Feet (in All Directions)	148	180	Stride frequency on first step	Basic	Agility ladder	
Reactive Push-Ups With Clap	154	186	Upper-body power and reaction to stimulus	Advanced		
Rope-Skipping	134	166	Lower-body quickness and elastic strength	Basic	Jump rope	
Ruler Drop Test	153	185	Upper-body quickness Reaction to stimulus	Basic	Ruler	
Scissor Jumps	136	168	Hip quickness Balance	Intermediate		
Sequence Jumping Jacks	147	179	Lower-body power and quickness	Intermediate		
Stability-Ball Cyclic Impact Lockouts	120	153	Core strength Absorbing impact	Advanced	Stability ball	
Stability-Ball Hops	121	154	Quickness in upper-body pushing musculature	Advanced	Stability ball	
Standing Long Jump	140	172	Lower-body power	Basic		
Three-Point Fire Drill With Reaction	162	194	Lower-body quickness Reaction Changing direction	Intermediate	Hoops	
Three-Step Foot-Tap Drill With Sprint	161	193	First-step quickness Reaction	Intermediate	Hoop, cone	
Three-Step Foot-Tap Drill With Sprint Plus Ball Drop	163	195	First-step quickness Upper-body reaction	Advanced	Hoop, tennis ball	
Triangle Drills With Commands	160	192	Foot plant quickness Changing direction	Intermediate	Cones	
Upper-Body Box Shuffles	132	165	Power and quickness in upper-body pushing musculature	Intermediate	Box or step	
Upper-Body Shuffles	129	162	Quickness in upper-body pushing musculature	Intermediate		●
Vertical Jump	139	171	Lower-body quickness and explosive power	Basic		
Wheelbarrow Drill	122	155	Upper-body and core power	Intermediate		
REACTION TIME						
Backpedal and Cut on Command	170	201	Mental processing speed Quickness of movement time Changing direction	Advanced		●
Backward Icky Shuffle With Reaction	192	219	Mental processing speed Court sense Total-body reaction time and agility General athleticism	Advanced	Agility ladder	
Backward Roll to Reaction	188	215	Mental processing speed Total-body reaction time and agility	Intermediate		

Name	Drill #	Page #	Emphasis	Level	Equipment	Shown on DVD
Ball Release	179	210	Mental processing speed Upper-body reaction time Quickness	Basic	Tennis balls	
Barrel Roll to Reaction	187	215	Mental processing speed Total-body reaction time and agility	Interme-diate		
The Bob	181	212	Mental processing speed Upper-body reaction time Total-body quickness	Interme-diate	Foam bat, focus mitt, or oversized boxing glove	
Card-Snatching	180	211	Upper-body quickness Reaction to visual stimuli	Basic	Playing card	
Chubby Checkers With Reaction	195	222	Mental processing speed Court sense Total-body reaction time First-step quickness General athleticism	Interme-diate	Agility ladder	
Directional Foot Movement	165	196	Mental processing speed First-step movement time	Basic		
Directional Hand Movement	166	197	Mental processing speed Upper-body movement time	Basic		
Directional Mirror Drill	167	198	Mental processing speed Quickness of movement time	Interme-diate		
Dodge Ball	185	214	Mental processing speed Total-body reaction time to visual stimuli	Interme-diate	Soft balls	
Drop-and-Go Pop-Up	176	207	Mental processing speed Total-body agility Kinesthetic awareness Quickness	Advanced	Ball	
Focus Mitt	184	213	Mental processing speed Upper-body reaction time Hand–eye coordination Total-body quickness	Interme-diate	Focus mitt	
Four-Point Pop-Up	172	203	Mental processing speed Total-body agility Kinesthetic awareness Quickness	Interme-diate		
Hop-Scotch With Reaction	190	217	Mental processing speed Court sense Total-body reaction time and agility General athleticism Ankle elastic strength	Interme-diate	Agility ladder	
Hot Hands	178	209	Mental processing speed Upper-body reaction time Quickness	Interme-diate		
Icky Shuffle With Reaction	191	218	Mental processing speed Court sense Total-body reaction time and agility General athleticism	Advanced	Agility ladder	

Name	Drill #	Page #	Emphasis	Level	Equipment	Shown on DVD
In-and-Out Shuffle With Reaction	193	220	Mental processing speed Court sense Total-body reaction time and agility General athleticism	Advanced	Agility ladder	●
Lying-to-Stand Pop-Up	174	205	Mental processing speed Total-body agility Kinesthetic awareness Quickness	Interme-diate		●
The Parry	182	212	Mental processing speed Upper-body reaction time Total-body quickness	Interme-diate	Foam bat, focus mitt, or oversized boxing glove	
Rapid Fire Interme-diate	186	214	Mental processing speed Total-body reaction time and quickness	Interme-diate		
Side-Shuffle	177	208	Mental processing speed Lateral agility Quickness	Interme-diate		
Sit-to-Stand Pop-Up	173	204	Mental processing speed Total-body agility Kinesthetic awareness Quickness	Interme-diate		
Skiers With Reaction	189	216	Mental processing speed Court sense Total-body reaction time and agility General athleticism	Advanced	Agility ladder	
Snake With Reaction	194	221	Mental processing speed Court sense Total-body reaction time and agility General athleticism Ankle elastic strength	Advanced	Agility ladder	
Sprawl-to-Stand Pop-Up	175	206	Mental processing speed Total-body agility Kinesthetic awareness Quickness	Interme-diate		
Sprint and Backpedal on Command	168	199	Reaction time Changing direction	Advanced		●
Sprint and Cut on Command	169	200	Mental processing speed Quickness of movement time Changing direction	Interme-diate		
Star Drill	171	202	Mental processing speed Multidirectional quickness	Basic	Hoops	
The Weave	183	213	Mental processing speed Upper-body reaction time Total-body quickness	Basic	Foam bat, focus mitt, or oversized boxing glove	

About the Editors

Lee E. Brown, EdD, CSCS*D, FACSM, is a certified strength and conditioning specialist (CSCS) through the National Strength and Conditioning Association (NSCA) and a previous member of the NSCA board of directors. He is also a certified health fitness instructor through the American College of Sports Medicine (ACSM) and a certified club coach through USA Weightlifting (USAW). In 2003 Brown received the NSCA Outstanding Young Investigator award for his research on high-velocity exercise.

Brown holds both a master's degree in exercise science and a doctorate in educational leadership from Florida Atlantic University. Formerly a high school physical education teacher and coach of many sports, Brown is now an associate professor of kinesiology in the department of kinesiology at California State University at Fullerton. He and his wife, Theresa, reside in Buena Park, California.

Vance A. Ferrigno, CSCS*D, is the director of fitness and aquatics at Woodfield Country Club in Boca Raton, Florida. In addition, he has been a strength and conditioning consultant to professional and amateur athletes since 1990. He is certified through ACSM as a health fitness instructor (HFI) as well as a health fitness director. He is also a certified strength and conditioning specialist through the NSCA and a USAWF club coach. Ferrigno, who earned his bachelor's degree in exercise science from Florida State University, assists in developing and teaching the curriculum for a strength and conditioning course at Florida Atlantic University. He resides in Coconut Creek, Florida.

About the Contributors

John Graham, MS, CSCS*D, is the vice president of rehabilitation and human performance at Orthopaedic Associates of Allentown (Pennsylvania), where he plans, organizes, and implements fitness, sports conditioning, and postrehabilitation programs for clients. He is a certified strength and conditioning specialist through the National Strength and Conditioning Association (NSCA), an ACSM-certified health fitness instructor, and USA Weightlifting level I coach. Graham is currently a column editor for the NSCA's *Strength & Conditioning Journal*. In addition to working with numerous high school programs and individual athletes, he has served as the strength coach and consultant for the U.S. national sprint cycling team (1995-2000, 2004) and for the Parkettes gymnastics team since 1995. Graham holds a master of science degree in health and physical education from East Stroudsburg University of Pennsylvania.

Andrew Hardyk, PhD, is the assistant track coach at Penn State University and has been on the Nittany Lion staff since 1995. He coaches the long, high, and triple jumpers, sprinters, and hurdlers. He also serves as the short relays coordinator. Hardyk coached athletes to All-American honors on 12 occasions and assisted in the development of three-time All-American decathlete James Cook. Hardyk has coached four additional NCAA qualifiers, and his athletes have set five Penn State records during his tenure. Hardyk received his bachelor's degree in aerospace engineering in 1992 and a master's degree in engineering mechanics the following year from the University of Cincinnati. In 2000 he received his PhD in sports biomechanics from Penn State University.

Doug Lentz, CSCS*D, is the director of fitness and wellness for Chambersburg Health Services in Chambersburg, Pennsylvania. Since receiving his BS degree from Penn State University in 1981, Lentz has trained adolescent, high school, college, Olympic, and professional athletes in 16 sports. Currently, he serves as the volunteer strength and conditioning coach for the Penn State women's tennis team and assists the Shippensburg University sprinters and middle-distance runners in their strength and power training. Lentz was the Pennsylvania state director for the National Strength and Conditioning Association (NSCA) from 1992 to 1998 and served as the chairperson for the NSCA Conference Committee from 1994 to 2004. He is now conference and special projects coordinator for the NSCA. Lentz is a USA Weightlifting (USAW) club coach and has completed course work and testing for the USAW senior coach course. He has served on the editorial board for the American Running Association since 1991.

Joshua Miller, MS, CSCS, NSCA-CPT, earned his master of science degree in exercise physiology at Florida Atlantic University. He holds certifications as a health/fitness instructor through the American College of Sports Medicine (ACSM-HFI) and strength and conditioning specialist (CSCS) and personal trainer with the National Strength and Conditioning Association (NSCA-CPT). He is certified as a club coach with the United States Cycling Federation. Miller is currently employed as the assistant director of clinical services with Metabolic Testing Services, LLC, based in Atlanta, Georgia.

Daniel Murray, MS, PT, CSCS, is a certified strength and conditioning specialist (CSCS) through the National Strength and Conditioning Association (NSCA) and a licensed physical therapist. As a physical therapist, Murray specializes in the treatment of orthopedic and sports-related disorders. He holds a master of science degree in kinesiology from California State University at Fullerton, where he is also involved in research performed in the movement analysis laboratory. Murray resides in Huntington Beach, California.

Steven Plisk, MS, CSCS*D, is the sports performance director at Velocity Sports Performance in Fairfield County, Connecticut. He received his bachelor of science degree in sport and exercise science from the State University of New York at Buffalo and his master of science in kinesiology from the University of Colorado. He has 15 years of experience in collegiate strength and conditioning and is currently an associate editor for the *Strength and Conditioning Journal.* Plisk is also a chapter author for the National Strength and Conditioning Association (NSCA) certification commission's *Essentials of Strength Training and Conditioning* as well as a presenter for the NSCA's educational symposia and Perform Better functional training seminars.

Jim Roberts, MS, CSCS, is certified as a strength and conditioning specialist (CSCS) through the National Strength and Conditioning Association (NSCA), as a specialist in biomechanics of resistance training through The Cooper Institute, and as a club coach through the United States Weightlifting Federation. Roberts is a continuing education provider for the NSCA, the National Athletic Trainers' Association (NATA), the National Academy of Sports Medicine (NASM), the American Council on Exercise (ACE), and several state boards for physical therapy. He has been a strength and conditioning coach for Baylor University, Lynn University, the Chris Evert Tennis Academy, and numerous high school volleyball programs including nationally ranked Olympic Heights High School. As a consultant, Roberts lectures extensively on functional training and human performance. He holds a master of science degree in exercise physiology from Florida Atlantic University and a bachelor of science in health and fitness from Baylor University.

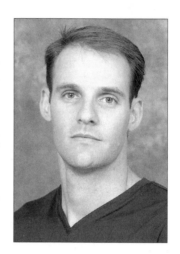

Diane Vives, CSCS*D, is the president of Vives Training Systems, a sports training and fitness company based in Austin, Texas. Vives holds a bachelor's degree in exercise science and wellness from Florida Atlantic University and holds certifications as a strength and conditioning specialist (CSCS) through the National Strength and Conditioning Association (NSCA), a health/fitness instructor by the American College of Sports Medicine (ACSM-HFI), a level I coach by USA Weightlifting, and a level I coach by USA Track and Field. Currently, she lectures to several nationally recognized organizations and has developed a DVD series on performance-enhancement education for training professionals and coaches. Vives also serves as the Southwest regional coordinator for the National Strength and Conditioning Association and is a member of the Sports Science Committee of the United States Tennis Association: Texas Section.

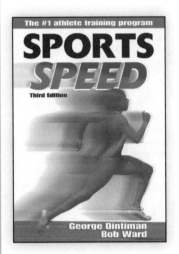
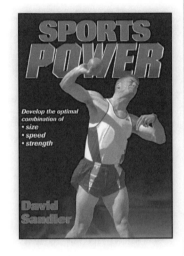